英语 2 单元过关检测

主　编　唐正林
副主编　胡　鑫　王　倩
参　编　李　芳　刘明绍　邹　茜　刘　婷　周文彬
　　　　　熊寒春　廖　星　王　端　陈兵武　庞启娟
　　　　　杜　晶　高芬远　黄银华　魏春辉　赵立英

版权专有　侵权必究

图书在版编目（CIP）数据

英语 2 单元过关检测 / 唐正林主编. -- 北京：北京理工大学出版社，2024.6.
ISBN 978-7-5763-4227-7

Ⅰ. G634.413

中国国家版本馆 CIP 数据核字第 2024J22G5 号

责任编辑：王晓莉	文案编辑：王晓莉
责任校对：周瑞红	责任印制：边心超

出版发行 / 北京理工大学出版社有限责任公司
社　　址 / 北京市丰台区四合庄路 6 号
邮　　编 / 100070
电　　话 / (010) 68914026（教材售后服务热线）
　　　　　(010) 68944437（课件资源服务热线）
网　　址 / http://www.bitpress.com.cn
版 印 次 / 2024 年 6 月第 1 版第 1 次印刷
印　　刷 / 定州启航印刷有限公司
开　　本 / 889 mm×1194 mm　1/8
印　　张 / 6.5
字　　数 / 134 千字
定　　价 / 28.50 元

图书出现印装质量问题，请拨打售后服务热线，负责调换

前 言

本书依据《中等职业学校英语课程标准》(2020年版)编写，按照课程标准要求，全面贯彻党的教育方针，践行社会主义核心价值观，落实立德树人根本任务，培育英语学科核心素养；立足中等职业教育实际和学生身心发展规律，进一步激发出学生的英语学习兴趣，使其掌握英语基础知识和基本技能，并为以后的职业生涯和终身发展打下坚实基础。

在编写过程中，我们的设计理念如下：

1. 立足教材，夯实基础知识

本书以教材单元教学为依据，挖掘每个单元的基础知识，紧扣教材编写相应的练习，帮助学生有效学习知识并拓展提高综合能力。

2. 围绕话题，拓展语用能力

本书紧扣教材单元教学话题，编写有效的阅读材料和书面表达任务，提升学生的语篇意识和思维能力，进而增强其阅读能力和语言应用能力。

3. 紧扣课标，提升核心素养

本书坚持以培养学科核心素养为宗旨，兼顾职业特色和价值导向，创设真实情境，引导学生形成正确的价值观。

本书在编写过程中，邀请了众多长期从事中等职业教育教学研究工作的专家和一线教师参与，题型设计合理，对中等职业学校学生非常实用。但是由于时间有限，资深专家参考，内容丰富，难免存在不足之处，肯请广大读者提出宝贵意见和建议，以便于修订完善。

编 者

目 录

Unit 1 单元测试 ……………………………………………………………… (1—4)

Unit 2 单元测试 ……………………………………………………………… (1—4)

Unit 3 单元测试 ……………………………………………………………… (1—4)

Unit 4 单元测试 ……………………………………………………………… (1—4)

期中检测题 …………………………………………………………………… (1—6)

Unit 5 单元测试 ……………………………………………………………… (1—4)

Unit 6 单元测试 ……………………………………………………………… (1—4)

Unit 7 单元测试 ……………………………………………………………… (1—4)

Unit 8 单元测试 ……………………………………………………………… (1—6)

期末检测题 …………………………………………………………………… (1—6)

参考答案

Unit 1 单元测试

一、根据首字母或中文意思完成句子。（5 小题，每题 1 分）

1. The man who has rich teaching e_____ is our teacher.
2. The p_____ has filled a gap in the market.
3. Everyone's fingerprints are _____ (唯一的).
4. We can call the hotel and make a r_____.
5. On arriving home I d_____ they had gone.

二、从方框中选择正确的短语并用正确的形式填空。（5 小题，每题 2 分）

| due to | all sorts of | set off | scenic spot | pass through |

6. Could you _____ the gate again?
7. It was raining heavily when they _____ for the valley.
8. They tried _____ methods to protect wild animals.
9. The accident was _____ excessive speed.
10. The lake has been a _____ for a long time.

三、单项选择。（10 小题，每题 1 分）

11. ————he _____ a good rest? —No he didn't.
    A. Do; had   B. Did; have   C. Did; had   D. Was; had
12. As soon as she _____, she _____ her a letter.
    A. arrived; writes   B. arrived; written
    C. arrived; wrote   D. arrived; write
13. Mr Smith was late because he _____ his way.
    A. losted   B. lose   C. loses   D. lost
14. Einstein _____ his Theory of Relativity.
    A. is famous as   B. was famous for
    C. is famous   D. was famous as
15. He's trying to _____ smoking.
    A. give up   B. gave up   C. giving up   D. given up
16. She _____ me when I was a baby.
    A. took care of   B. take care of
    C. look after   D. looks after
17. It was sunny. He suggested _____ out for a walk.
    A. going   B. to go   C. goes   D. go
18. What _____ they _____ dinner yesterday?
    A. do; have for   B. did; had for
    C. did; have for   D. were; have for
19. Li Fang _____ 50 yuan for the lost library book.
    A. paid   B. spent   C. pay   D. lost
20. When _____ Jim _____ school this morning?
    A. did; get to   B. did; got
    C. did; got to   D. did; get

四、语言应用。（5 小题，每题 2 分）

21. Mr Green wants to send a package. He can't send it in _____.
    A. an envelope   B. a box   C. an e-mail
22. What do you think FUSION GRILL is?

— 1 —

23. When can we go for a picnic?
A. A cinema.   B. A restaurant.   C. A shop.

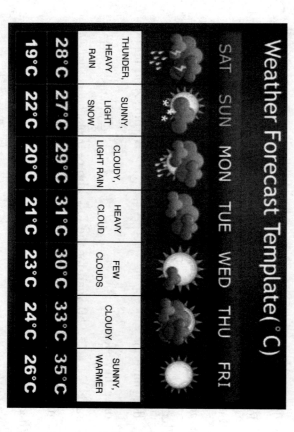

24. You can scan this picture when you want to _____ on mobile phone.
A. On Saturday.   B. On Tuesday.   C. On Friday.

A. buy something   B. chat with your friends
C. rent a car

25. The color of the product is _____.
A. white   B. red   C. black

五、阅读理解。（15 小题，每题 2 分）

A

The spaceship and three astronauts of the Shenzhou XIII task were successfully sent to the Tiāngong space station on October 16, 2021. The members of China's Shenzhou XIII task, Wang Yaping, Zhai Zhigang and Ye Guangfu, gave a lecture to students around the world on December 9, 2021. This was the first try of it. Millions of students across China watched the beginning of Tiāngong Classroom. The second Tiāngong Classroom was on March 23, 2022. Certainly, they were special, interesting and fantastic lectures all over the world.

Wang Yaping also took part in the Shenzhou X task that lasted nearly 15 days on June 11, 2013. During that task, she carried out the nation's first space-based lecture to Chinese students on June 20, 2013. The activity made China, following the United States, the second country to have held a space-based class for students.

In the future, Tiāngong Classroom will encourage more young people to study science and technology and learn something more about the space.

26. What does the underlined word "**it**" refer to?
A. Shenzhou X.   B. Tiāngong Classroom.
C. Shenzhou XIII.   D. Tiāngong space station.

27. What's the correct order for the following events about Wang Yaping?
① She took part in the 15-day Shenzhou X task.
② She was successfully sent to Tiāngong space station.
③ She carried out the nation's first space-based lecture in the Shenzhou X.
④ She and the other two astronauts gave a lecture to students around the world.
A. ①③②④   B. ①④③②   C. ③④①②   D. ③④②①

28. What's the purpose of Tiāngong Classroom?
A. To give special, interesting and fantastic lectures to the astronauts.
B. To carry out the nation's space-based lecture to American students.
C. To make China the second country to hold a space-based class.
D. To encourage students to learn about science, technology and space.

29. In which part of the newspaper can the passage be found?
A. School Time.   B. Sports News.
C. Science Study.   D. Outdoor Fun.

30. How many countries have held a space-based class so far?
A. 1.   B. 2.   C. 3.   D. 4.

B

I don't know what's wrong with my brain. My memory started to become shockingly complete in 1974, when I was eight years old. From 1980 on, it has been near-perfect. Give me a date from that year forward, and I can immediately tell you what day of the week it was, what I did on that day, and what happened on that day.

I can recall memories at will. But my remembering, in fact, is not under my control. My memories automatically(自动地) flash forward and backward in my head through the years of my life. What does it feel like? Well, just imagine this: Someone started to make videos of you when you were a child, and has been continuously following you around all day, every day. This person has placed all of these videos onto a single DVD, and you are being forced to watch it over and over again. There you are as a ten-year-old in your living room watching your favorite TV program. Then, suddenly, you're on the beach during a family vacation when you were twelve. I never know what I might remember next.

As I grew up, a great many new memories were being stored in my brain, with more and more of them endlessly flashing through my mind. I became a prisoner of my own memory. My mother would tell me not to care so much about the past. I'd try to explain that I didn't really care about the past. The memories just flooded my mind. But nobody could understand me.

My greatest hope now is that scientists will discover something about my brain in the near future. I hope their findings will help them learn more about the human mind.

31. The writer's special ability became almost perfect when she was _____ years old.
A. 8   B. 10   C. 12   D. 14

32. We can learn from the text that the writer _____.
A. cannot tell one person from another
B. cannot remember anything about the past
C. can say what will happen in the near future
D. can recall what exactly happened on each past day

33. How did the writer feel about her special ability?
A. Proud.   B. Warm.   C. Painful.   D. Shameful.

34. The writer's mother _____.
A. knew what was wrong with her brain
B. couldn't understand her problem
C. cared little about the past
D. solved her problem

35. The writer now hopes scientists will _____.
A. discover her amazing ability
B. help her become a normal person
C. explain the mystery and control her memories
D. study her brain to learn more about the human mind

C

Here is a story: A man sees a butterfly(蝴蝶) trying to get out of its chrysalis(蛹) with difficulty. Feeling sorry for it, the man decides to help. He cuts the chrysalis and the butterfly comes out easily. Surprisingly enough, the butterfly is unable to fly. If the butterfly doesn't struggle (挣扎) to leave the chrysalis, it can't fly! The struggle develops the energy in the butterfly which makes it fly. Similarly, the challenges of life bring out the best in young people and make them fly.

When people are young, meeting and overcoming challenges will make them strong and ready to face life. When we look at successful people, we see that the most successful of them are people who have had to struggle. One famous businessman, who now owns many big supermarkets, used to carry clothes on his back and sell them from door to door when he was young. Another successful man is Dennis. His father died when he was only twenty. His father's death forced him to mature fast. He had to bring up a family of nine people. He took up the challenges and overcame them. Today his brothers and sisters are leading successful lives.

Sometimes challenges do not appear to us because we keep away from them. So some parents and teachers actively encourage young people to face challenges. They might organize some activities for young people which provide them with challenges, like rock-climbing, camping, volunteer work and so on. However, just passing exams will not prepare a person for life. We must meet and overcome challenges. The young people of today will become the leaders of tomorrow. For countries to continue to become successful, it is important that the young people learn to meet challenges and overcome them.

36. From the story we know that the butterfly can't fly because _____.
A. it gets out by itself   B. the man feels sorry for it
C. it tries to challenge itself   D. the man helps it come out

37. Dennis's example shows that successful people should _____.
A. take on challenges   B. take up business early
C. lead successful lives   D. learn to bring up a family

38. The meaning of the underlined word "mature" in the passage is _____.
A. wake up   B. give up   C. grow up   D. bring up

39. According to the passage, _____.
A. challenges always appear to everyone
B. passing exams don't belong to challenges
C. rock-climbing and camping are helpful challenges
D. it's unnecessary for young people to do volunteer challenges

40. What is the purpose of the passage?
A. To describe where a butterfly comes from.
B. To encourage young people to face challenges.
C. To suggest how to become a successful businessman.
D. To tell what will happen if a person fails.

六、把左右栏相对应的句子匹配起来。（5小题，每题1分）

41. Have a good summer holiday!   A. Neither. It's on Martin Street.
42. Is the Maple Leaf Hotel on Maple Street or   B. Me too.
    Craven Street?   C. Thanks. The same to you.
43. I like Chinese food.   D. It will clear up.
44. What's your hobby, Linda?   E. I love travelling most.
45. What will the weather be like this afternoon?

七、英汉互译。（15小题，每题2分）

46. The boy is searching for local scenic spots on the Internet.

47. The upper part of the mountains is covered by snow all year round.

48. I can't wait to visit Jiuzhaigou Valley.

49. She loves freedom and hopes to explore the nature.

50. Can I use credit cards to buy tickets on the machine?

51. At the age of 17, Marco Polo set out for his first trip.

52. 真的很值得一游。
It's really _____.

53. 徐霞客花了30多年周游全国。
Xu Xiake _____ over 30 years _____ throughout the country.

54. 我每天早晨通常要花费一个小时练习瑜伽。
It usually _____ me an hour _____ practice Yoga every morning.

55. 我期待着见到您。
We are _____ seeing you.

56. 我对中国和中国食物很感兴趣。

57. 你能告诉我更多关于这个城市的事情吗?

58. 你愿意加入我们吗?

59. 去年我们经常乘公共汽车去上学。

60. 你应该先做一个旅行计划。

Unit 2 单元测试

一、根据首字母或中文意思完成句子。(5小题，每题1分)

1. The a_____ is at 5 p.m.
2. Thinking positively is one way of dealing with s_____.
3. He is in bed with a t_____ of 40℃.
4. Giving up smoking can _____ (减少) the risk of heart disease.
5. It's a waste of time and _____ (精力).

二、从方框中选择正确的短语并用正确的形式填空。(5小题，每题2分)

| suffer from | as a result | burn off | give sb. a hand | lose one's temper |

6. She died _____ of heart disease.
7. A lot of students _____ learning pressure.
8. The man _____ and shouted at the woman.
9. Jogging every day can help you _____ calories.
10. I _____ if you are in trouble.

三、单项选择。(10小题，每题1分)

11. My work is _____ the baby.
    A. look after   B. looks after
    C. looked after   D. to look after
12. In summer, the food goes _____ easily.
    A. badly   B. bad   C. good   D. well
13. The weather _____ colder and colder.
    A. is going   B. becoming   C. is getting   D. growing
14. If you go to Tibet, you _____ its beautiful scenery.
    A. will fall in love with   B. fall in love with
    C. fall in love   D. falling in love with
15. His father _____ for five years.
    A. has died   B. dead   C. has been dead   D. died
16. —Have you read today's newspaper?
    —Yes. It's really boring. There is _____ in it.
    A. new nothing   B. new anything
    C. nothing new   D. something new
17. I have read all the books _____ you gave me.
    A. it   B. which   C. this   D. that
18. —Please remember the words in this lesson.
    —Yes, and I will _____ in my notebook.
    A. write down it   B. write down them
    C. write them down   D. write it down
19. If you are in trouble, you can _____ help from the policeman.
    A. ask for   B. think about   C. warm up   D. look over
20. You must wear glasses. They can keep your eyes _____.
    A. save   B. safe   C. safely   D. to see

四、语言应用。(5小题，每题2分)

21. The lowest temperature is on _____.
    A. Sunday   B. Saturday   C. Wednesday

22. The function of this tablets is to _____

23. 4. This instruction is _____.
A. help nighttime sleep   B. sleep well in the daytime   C. keep awake

24. Which of the following is right?
A. to teach you how to take the medicine
B. to help you how to operate the machine
C. to teach you how to write an instruction

25. The sign means that _____.
A. Place it on the table.   B. Take it after drinking.
C. take it 3 times a day.

五、阅读理解。（15 小题，每题 2 分）

A

Room Type	Room Rate (Yuan)
Standard Room	588
Deluxe King Room	788
Executive VIP Room	988
Business Suite	1388
Executive Suite	1688
VIP-Suite	3888
Extra Bed	200

Tips:
1. Check-out time is 12:30p.m., late check-out by 6:00p.m. You need to pay more 100 Yuan.
2. Need to advance rent when you check in.
3. All major credit cards are accepted.
No. 2 Nanjing Road, Shanghai
Tel：1234567 6543
E-mail：sunshinehotel@123.cn

26. If Mary and her friends book a standard room at first, then add a bed, they should pay _____ Yuan.
A. 788   B. 588   C. 688   D. 988

27. The Sunshine Hotel is in _____.
A. London   B. Yunnan   C. Shanghai   D. Nanjing

28. Lily wants to book a room, she can't contact the hotel _____.
A. by e-mail   B. by letter

C. by fax   D. by telephone
29. Lily stayed in an Executive VIP Room last night, she checked out at 7:50p.m. today, she will pay _____ yuan.
    A. 1,088   B. 988   C. 1,188   D. 1,288
30. You can see this form _____.
    A. in a hotel   B. in a restaurant
    C. in a museum   D. in a classroom

B

1. Eating healthy food does not always mean that eating fancy foods or salad but eating right food and at the right time is considered.
2. We should eat green vegetables for good health as green vegetables are rich in antioxidants and vitamins.
3. Water is an essential part of our life. We should drink at least 8-9 glasses of water everyday.
4. Sleeping is important for our body as proper sleep can relax our mind and maintains peace of mind. We should sleep at least 6-7 hours daily.
5. Doing exercise daily can make the body fit from fat and make the body healthy.
6. Smoking may affect lungs, heart, brain and causes cancer. Once you become addicted to it, then it won't be easy to get out of this trap.
7. If you won't keep yourself clean and tidy, the germs will reach to our stomach and cause many problems or viral infection.

31. Which of the following is NOT true?
    A. We should drink at least eight or nine glasses of water daily.
    B. We should sleep at least four or five hours daily.
    C. It won't be easy to give up smoking if you become addicted to it.
    D. Green vegetables are rich in antioxidants and vitamins.
32. How many ways can we stay healthy according to the passage?
    A. Eight.   B. Seven.   C. Six.   D. Nine.
33. Which is NOT correct way to keep healthy?
    A. Eating green vegetables.   B. Eating healthy food.
    C. Staying up late.   D. Doing exercise daily.
34. We can use "_____" to replace the underlined word "essential".
    A. difficult   B. interesting   C. important   D. necessary
35. The passage is mainly about _____.
    A. how to keep healthy   B. how to eat
    C. how to sleep well   D. smoking

C

"Set a goal". Are you familiar with these words? Of course. Every time you want to do something, people will advise you to set a goal. The following tips may help you.

Spend some time thinking about exactly what results you wish to achieve and be as specific as you can. Establish a time frame for achieving each part of your final goal.

Set your sights on a goal that is reasonable to accomplish. As you set your goal, ask yourself not only what you want to accomplish, but why you want to accomplish it. Figuring out what drives your goal will help you plan in the beginning, and interest as you move toward your target. If you want to lose weight, for example, your reasons may include wanting to feel more comfortable in your own skin, be more physically capable, and feel better about your appearance.

Write down your goal on an easy-to-see place, such as your wall calendar.

36. According to this passage, what should you do first if you want to learn a foreign language?
    A. Buy a book.   B. Set a goal.
    C. Spend time thinking about it.   D. Ask yourself some questions.
37. In paragraph 3, why do people want to lose weight?
    A. Because you want to feel less comfortable.
    B. Because you want to be less capable in physics.
    C. Because you want to look better.
    D. Because you are too fat.
38. How many tips are given in the passage above?
    A. 3.   B. 4.   C. 5.   D. 2.
39. To set a reasonable goal, you can _____.
    A. think about the reason   B. ask yourself what to accomplish
    C. figure out what drives you   D. all above
40. The passage is mainly about _____.
    A. how to set a reasonable goal

— 3 —

B. the importance of setting a goal
C. writing down your goal
D. how to stick to a goal

六、把左右栏相对应的句子匹配起来。（5小题，每题1分）

41. What are they doing?	A. I was at home.
42. Where were you during the holiday?	B. Thanks.
43. Welcome to my party.	C. They are painting a sandcastle.
44. Would you like a cup of tea?	D. Four.
45. How many seasons are there in a year?	E. No, thanks. I'd like a glass of water.

46. My hometown is famous for its beautiful scenery and delicious food.

47. It never rains but it pours.

48. If you want to get close to nature, you are sure to fall in love with Yunnan.

49. I have a sore throat and a terrible cough.

50. You should avoid heavy food.

51. Exercise can reduce people's risk of suffering from stress and depression.

52. 我什么时候能康复？
When can I _____ ?

53. 还有其他什么我需要注意的吗？
What else should I _____ ?

54. 你可以用你的智能手机预约。
You can _____ with your smart phone.

55. 你看上去气色不好。
You don't _____ .

七、英汉互译。（15小题，每题2分）

56. 众所周知，好的健康比财富更重要。

57. 过马路时要小心。

58. 这张床对他来说够大了。

59. 散步对你的健康来说是必不可少的。

60. 他经常陷入麻烦中。

Unit 3 单元测试

一、根据首字母或中文意思完成句子。（5小题，每题1分）

1. Mary really wants to be an a_____ secretary during her internship.
2. How did you get along well with your c_____?
3. Huaxia company's m_____ will give all the interns a speech on the internship program.
4. The best intern will get our company's s_____.
5. As an intern, communicating with real guests is a big c_____.

二、从方框中选择正确的短语并用正确的形式填空。（5小题，每题2分）

be absent from   keep tack of   instead of   go through   deal with

6. As an intern, it's hard for me to _____ after-sales problems.
7. My friends _____ the welcome meeting yesterday.
8. We should try our best to solve these problems _____ complaining.
9. Our mentor will also _____ our internship practice.
10. Let's _____ the numbers together and see if a workable deal is possible.

三、单项选择。（10小题，每题1分）

11. —Was she talking with the training teacher?
    —_____.
    A. Yes, she was.   B. Yes, she is.
    C. No, she was.   D. No, she isn't.

12. What _____ you _____ just now?
    A. was; doing   B. were; doing   C. are; doing   D. will; do

13. Mary was walking into the classroom _____ the bell rang.
    A. while   B. where   C. when   D. though

14. We will _____ the precious opportunity _____ you if you pass the test.
    A. offer; with   B. provide; with   C. supply; with   D. offer; to

15. I will feel _____ and _____ at the real workplace.
    A. confidence; skillful   B. confident; skillful
    C. confidence; skill   D. confident; skill

16. Let's _____ the paper and find out a solution.
    A. go through   B. go back   C. go ahead   C. go into

17. Susan _____ to turn off the tap last night.
    A. forget   B. forgets
    C. forgot   D. is forgetting

18. Lucy with her two friends _____ waiting at the reception desk when the manager came in.
    A. is   B. are   C. was   D. are

19. Not only you but also I _____ interested in the pre-service training program.
    A. are   B. do   C. does   D. am

20. Yang Lulu did well in the pre-service training session _____ get a scholarship offered by the company.
    A. as   B. in case   C. so that   D. so as to

四、语言应用。（5小题，每题2分）

21. Which public service is for kids?
    A. Prenatal Health Care.   B. Children's Health Care.
    C. Women's Health Care.

22. What can we infer according to the picture?
    A. They are at the supermarket.
    B. The economy in China is recovering.
    C. The confidence of consumers in China gets boost as economy recovers.

23. What kind of noodles are there in the three bowls?

This photo taken on April 5, 2023 shows three bowls of just-cooked Lamian noodles at a noodle restaurant run by Ma Xueming in Xining, Northwest China's Qinghai province.

A. Chongqing spicy noodles.　　B. Dragon beard noodles.
C. Lamian noodles.

24. Jacky Cheung is famous for _____.

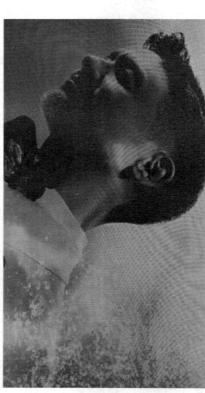

Jackcy Cheung set to launch new concert tour

A. dancing　　B. drawing　　C. singing

25. The enthusiasts are celebrate _____.

Hanfu lovers gather in Xixi Wetland in Hangzhou to celebrate coming of spring

A. Spring Festival　　B. Dragon Boat Festival
C. early spring

五、阅读理解。(15小题，每题 2 分)

A

The Nautilus expedition to the Cayman Islands

Day 1: August 15th

I'm one of five very lucky students-chosen to go on Nautilus's four-day expedition(探险) to the Cayman Islands. We had a talk from the expedition leader Dr. Katy Croft Bell, about where we're going and what we'll be doing. Oh, and all the safety rules as well, of course!

Day 2: August 16th

What an amazing day! In the morning, we met Dr. Robert Ballard, who discovered the wreck (残骸) of the Titanic! I even got a chance to guide the ship! Later we learned about Hercules. This robot is sent deep into the sea to look for shipwrecks, to study the plants and animals, and to look at the rocks in an area.

Day 3: August 17th

This morning we appeared on the Nautilus Live website and talked to students around the world about our expedition. It was amazing-I feel like a real famous person now! The afternoon was NOT cool, however. There was a big storm, and we all felt very seasick!

Day 4: August 18th

This morning was beautiful, and the sea was peaceful. Perfect for a dive (潜水). In the afternoon, we arrived at Grand Cayman. Although I'm sad to leave the Nautilus team (especially Hercules), I'm excited to explore(探索) the islands and the waters!

26. How did Talita feel about taking part in Nautilus's expedition to the Cayman Islands?
A. Surprised.　　B. Excited.
C. Worried.　　D. Doubtful.

27. What did Dr. Robert Ballard discover?
A. The wreck of Nautilus.　　B. The wreck of Cayman Islands.
C. The wreck of Hercules.　　D. The wreck of the Titanic.

28. What is the robot Hercules used for?
A. Giving diving shows.　　B. Exploring the deep sea.
C. Helping with lab work.　　D. Guiding tourists around the islands.

29. What did Talita do on Day 3?
A. She learned about the history of the Titanic.
B. She attended a speech from the expedition leader.
C. She shared her expedition with students worldwide.

D. She visited the place where the captain of Nautilus works.

30. What is the most suitable activity on Day 4?
A. Swimming. B. Diving.
C. Playing sand volleyball. D. Sunbath.

B

In March 2017, about 25 people were invited to a kitchen in San Francisco, California, for a tasting event. "This is some of the best fried chicken I've had," one guest said.

The compliment was extra special considering the meat had been grown in a lab by scientists from Memphis Meats. The company makes meat by safely taking cells(细胞) from animals such as chickens and cows. Those cells grow to meat.

The world's population is expected to grow to nearly 10 billion by 2050, according to the United Nations Food and Agriculture Organization (FAO). Eric Schulze is a vice president at Memphis Meats. Schulze said, "With current meat production methods, there are not enough resources(资源) such as land and water to meet that need."

Traditional meat production also requires lots of cows. And cows produce methane(沼气). This gas traps heat in the atmosphere, resulting in climate(气候) change. Raising cows and other livestock(牲畜) takes up space, too. But cellular-meat production requires fewer cows and less land. "You only need the land required for the facilities(设施) where the meat is made," said Elliot, a scientist at the Good Food Institute.

Alison researches animal science at the University of California. She points out that fossil fuels (化石燃料), such as coal, are used to power cellular-meat production facilities. Burning these fuels produces another heat-trapping gas: CO_2. "If we're burning coal so that we can grow cellular meat," she asks, "are we going backward?"

31. What does the underlined word "compliment" in paragraph 2 probably mean?
A. 建议 B. 赞扬 C. 面试 D. 介绍

32. What does the author want to tell us in paragraph 3?
A. People will have to cut down their meat needs.
B. There will be a great need for meat in the future.
C. People will need to develop more resources like land.
D. The world's population will increase at a greater speed.

33. What advantage does cellular-meat production have according to paragraph 4?
A. It has lower cost. B. It takes less time.
C. It helps the environment. D. It improves the taste of meat.

34. Which statement is TRUE according to the passage?
A. Cellular meat is more delicious than the real meat.
B. The facilities do no harm to the environment.
C. Burning fossil fuels may result in the climate change.
D. Cellular meat is healthier than the real meat.

35. What's Alison attitude to cellular-meat production?
A. Doubtful. B. Humorous. C. Uninterested. D. Supportive.

C

My dad doesn't seem like the kind of guy who would bake(烤) great bread, but he is and he does.

The rest of the week, Dad fixes cars at work. The shop where Dad works doesn't have enough work. I think Dad began baking bread to help him relax.

I've been feeling kind of stressed out myself since I found out I didn't make the school swim team. Now I'll have to wait a whole year to try out again. Plus, I'm taking some difficult classes this year.

I think Dad knew I was feeling bad. He said it was time for me to help. Then he headed to the kitchen.

Dad got out his big mixing bowl, handed me a large wooden spoon, and told me to mix while he added the ingredients(原料). Dad isn't big on measuring. He knows how much of each ingredient to use, and the bread always turns out great.

When I finished stirring, Dad showed me how to knead the dough(揉面团). Next came the most difficult part-doing nothing. We put the dough back into the bowl and then we waited for more than three hours for the dough to slowly rise and double in size.

Dad said the waiting is always the hardest part. "It's hard to resist(抵制) putting the dough directly into the oven(烤箱), but if you do, the bread will be hard. The most important lesson of all is learning to be." Dad taught me more than how to bake bread.

36. What can we learn about the author's father?
A. He is living a relaxing life.
B. He tries his best to make ends meet.
C. He manages to balance work and life.
D. He is more like a baker than a mechanic.

37. Why is the author feeling stressed?
A. School isn't going well.

B. She dislikes making bread.
C. She feels sorry for her father.
D. Some classes aren't worth it.

38. What does the underlined sentence "Dad isn't big on measuring" in paragraph 5 mean?
A. Dad is unskilled.
B. Dad dislikes measuring.
C. Dad has a craze for measuring.
D. Dad is careful about ingredients.

39. Which statement is NOT true from the text?
A. The author is a schoolboy.
B. Both the author and his father meet difficulties in life.
C. The author are forced to bake bread by his father.
D. The father is an optimistic man.

40. What lesson has the author learned from her dad?
A. Never give up.
B. Take life easily.
C. Believe in yourself.
D. Enjoy time with family.

六、把左右栏相对应的句子匹配起来。（5小题，每题1分）

41. How is it going with your internship?	A. Of course!
42. How do you feel facing real guests?	B. So far, so good.
43. Do you get along well with your colleagues?	C. I can't work out the maths problems
44. What happened?	D. It was a challenge at the beginning.
45. What was she doing at the reception?	E. She was receiving some guests.

46. I was doing my homework when someone knocked at my door.

七、英汉互译。（15小题，每题2分）

47. Do not teach fish to swim.

48. While I was doing some cleaning, my sister was watching TV.

49. While the sun was shining, it wasn't very warm.

50. Tom was hit by a truck while crossing the street.

51. The assistant receptionist knew John because he often came to the company.

52. 华夏公司成立于1986年。
Huaxia Company _____ in 1986.

53. 如果实习生被录用了，请提供由学校教练及学生提供的三方协议。
If an intern is employed, please provide the _____ by the school, the trainer and the students.

54. 为了在华夏酒店实习，我需要先制定一个计划。
_____ take an _____ in Huaxia hotel, I need to make a plan first.

55. 这将帮助我在未来的职业生涯中取得更大进步。
This will help me _____ more _____ in my future career.

56. 你检查了你的保险吗？

57. 他们也会为国际生提供英语语言课程。

58. 这些课程提供了高水平的相关职业技能和知识。

59. 文凭一般需要一到两年的脱产学习。

60. 我完成了我的实习计划。

Unit 4 单元测试

一、根据首字母或中文意思完成句子。(5小题,每题1分)

1. It will take a week for your a＿＿＿＿ to be processed.
2. The winners were given an e＿＿＿ welcome when they arrived home.
3. K＿＿＿ is power.
4. The media should be more ＿＿＿＿(有责任心的) in what they report.
5. She now helps in a local school as a v＿＿＿ three days a week.

二、从方框中选择正确的短语并用正确的形式填空。(5小题,每题2分)

act as   be skilled in   major in   look forward to   home and abroad

6. Read books about great leaders from ＿＿＿＿.
7. We're really ＿＿＿＿ seeing you again.
8. This young girl ＿＿＿＿ arranging flowers.
9. One of the men stood at the door to ＿＿＿＿ a lookout.
10. I enjoyed studying English, so I decided to ＿＿＿＿ languages at college.

三、单项选择。(10小题,每题1分)

11. You need to hand in an ＿＿＿ form.
    A. apply   B. applied   C. application   D. applying
12. We must be patient ＿＿＿ children.
    A. with   B. over   C. in   D. on
13. I'm just ＿＿＿ university professor.
    A. an   B. a   C. /   D. on
14. I now look forward to ＿＿＿ to work as soon as possible.
    A. go back   B. went back   C. gone back   D. going back
15. I consider it important to have ＿＿＿ English.
    A. a good knowledge to   B. good knowledge of
    C. a good knowledge on   D. good knowledge on
16. What ＿＿＿ it is! It is a good idea to go outing.
    A. a fine weather   B. a terrible weather   C. terrible weather   D. fine weather
17. We'll ＿＿＿ the result soon.
    A. inform you   B. inform you of   C. inform of you   D. inform you with
18. ＿＿＿ amazing that film is!
    A. What   B. How   C. What a   D. How a
19. We stood up ＿＿＿ get a better view.
    A. in order that   B. on purpose   C. in order to   D. for purpose of
20. ＿＿＿ enthusiastic skier he is!
    A. What   B. How an   C. What a   D. What an

四、语言应用。(5小题,每题2分)

21. They are collecting ＿＿＿＿.
    A. water   B. plastic bottles   C. leaves

22. According to the sign, we can't ＿＿＿ here.
    A. climb   B. jump   C. run

— 1 —

23. The company party will last _____.
A. one hour
B. two hours
C. three hours

24. We can go to the Morgan Furniture Center at _____.
A. 5:00 p.m. on Saturday
B. 9:30 a.m. on Sunday
C. 1:30 p.m. on Tuesday

25. Who would like to perform can sign up for the talent show?
A. A parent.
B. A middle school student.
C. A middle school teacher.

五、阅读理解。（15小题，每题2分）

A

Would you travel halfway across the world by bus? Expedition company Adventures Overland is hoping you'll say yes to its new organized bus trip, which will take travelers from the Indian metropolis(首都) of Delhi to the UK capital of London-no airplanes involved. Described as the "first-ever hop-on/hop-off bus service" between the two destinations, bus to London will take 20 passengers on a modified luxury bus, inspired in part by the Hippie Trail buses that crisscrossed (往返于) the world in the 1950s and 1960s.

The bus will cross 18 countries over a period of 70 days, with passengers hopping off to admire the view at the pagodas of Myanmar, hike the Great Wall of China and wander historic cities including Moscow and Prague. This road trip doesn't come cheap-it will cost around $20,000—but you can choose to just do part of the journey, which is divided into four legs. The first Bus to London journey was set to take place in mid-2021.

26. The new organized bus trip ferries passengers to set out from _____.
A. Myanmar to Prague
B. Delhi to London
C. Prague to London
D. Moscow to China

27. The modified luxury bus was inspired in part by _____.
A. the Hippie Trail buses that crisscrossed the world in the 1950s and 1960s
B. the Hippie Trail buses that crisscrossed the world in the 1950 and 1960
C. "first-ever hop-on/hop-off bus service" between the two destinations
D. the view at the pagodas of Myanmar, the Great Wall of China and historic cities

28. It will take the bus _____ to cross 18 countries.
A. less than a month
B. nearly three months
C. over two months
D. nearly two months

29. The first Bus to London journey was set to take the road _____.
A. At the beginning of 2021
B. at the end of 2021
C. in the middle of 2021
D. in the 1960s

30. Which is the best title of the passage?
A. The New Organized Bus Trip
B. London Journey
C. The Hippie Trail Buses

C. The Latest Move to Charge Customers for Plastic Bags.
D. The Latest Move to Ban the Use of Non-degradable Plastic Bags in a Majority of Cities.

C

The Ministry of Education wants universities to strictly check the authenticity(真实性) of the nationality of prospective international students to close admission loopholes(漏洞).

The ministry issued a new rule on Wednesday targeting students who acquired foreign nationality by birth but have studied at Chinese primary and secondary schools and have at least one parent who is Chinese. Starting from next year, such students should have lived in a foreign country for more than two of the past four years to be able to apply to study at Chinese universities as international students.

The new overseas residency requirement for foreign-born students matches an existing requirement for students who have acquired foreign nationality through emigration. Those students also need to have held their foreign nationality for at least four years.

Yu Minhong, founder of education consultancy New Oriental Education and Technology Group, "Chinese students have to pass the national college entrance exam to enter Chinese universities, but international students have been admitted based on their test scores in high schools and the HSK exam, a Chinese language proficiency test. That has prompted some parents to give birth to their children overseas so they can bypass the gaokao," he said.

36. Starting from next year, the prospective international students should _____ to be able to apply to study at Chinese universities as international students, according to the passage.
A. have lived in China for more than two of the past four years
B. have lived in a foreign country for more than two of the past four years
C. have lived in a foreign country for more than two years
D. have lived in China for more than two of the past four years

37. Yu Minhong is _____.
A. a foreign-born student
B. an international student
C. the leader of The Ministry of Education
D. the founder of education consultancy New Oriental Education and Technology Group

38. The international students have been admitted based on _____.
A. their test scores in high schools and the HSK exam
B. their test scores in high schools only

— 3 —

D. Expedition company Adventures Overland

B

The National Development and Reform Commission, the Ministry of Ecology and Environment and seven other ministries jointly introduced a guiding document, which stated non-degradable(不可降解的) plastic bags would be banned in a majority of cities from Jan 1, 2021.

All supermarkets and stores are required to charge customers for plastic bags, but the latest move shows the authorities' determination to reduce white pollution by putting an end to the use of plastic bags altogether.

The move found widespread support on social networking sites, as more people are waking up to the importance of getting rid of plastic garbage. People who are <u>accustomed</u> to getting a plastic bag after buying goods in the supermarket will now have to look for degradable ones, if they are available.

Enterprises that produce non-degradable, disposable plastic bags will have to start producing degradable ones or go out of business.

31. How many ministries jointly introduced the guiding document banning non-degradable plastic bags?
A. 7. B. 8. C. 9. D. 10.

32. Many people on social networking sites are _____ the move of putting an end to the use of plastic bags according to the passage.
A. against with B. in favor of C. indifferent to D. opposed to

33. What does the underlined word "accustomed" mean in Paragraph 3?
A. 习惯于 B. 风俗 C. 依赖于 D. 希望

34. Which of the following is TRUE?
A. Non-degradable(不可降解的) plastic bags would be banned in a majority of cities from Jan 11, 2021.
B. Few people are waking up to the importance of getting rid of plastic garbage.
C. After buying goods in the supermarket people will not have to look for degradable ones, if they are available.
D. If they do not want to go out of business, enterprises that produce non-degradable, disposable plastic bags will turn to producing degradable ones.

35. What does the passage mainly talk about?
A. Non-degradable Plastic Bags.
B. Degradable Plastic Bags.

C. the HSK exam only
D. passing the national college entrance exam

39. According to the passage, why do some parents choose to give birth to their children overseas?
A. Because their children can pass the national college entrance exam.
B. Because their children can live a better life overseas.
C. Because their children can bypass the national college entrance exam.
D. Because their children can not bypass the gaokao.

40. Which of the following is NOT TRUE?
A. Chinese students have to pass the national college entrance exam to enter Chinese universities.
B. Foreign-born students who want to enter Chinese universities also need to have held their foreign nationality for at least four years.
C. The Ministry of Education wants universities to strictly check the authenticity of the nationality of prospective international students to close admission loopholes.
D. The ministry issued a new rule on Wednesday targeting students who acquired foreign nationality by birth but have studied in Chinese colleges and have at least one parent who is Chinese.

六、把左右栏相对应的句子匹配起来。（5小题，每题1分）

41. Have you done any volunteer work before?	A. It's my pleasure
42. What can you help with in the community?	B. I am a vocational school student. And I'm 16 years old.
43. Could you introduce yourself?	C. About 6 months.
44. Thank you for your help.	D. I can help people sort the garbage.
45. How long do you plan to stay at a rural elementary school?	E. Yes. I helped to collect some books and sent them to elementary schools.

七、英汉互译。（15小题，每题2分）

46. I major in Elementary Education in a university and I'll graduate in July.

47. With a history of over 600 years, the Palace Museum in Beijing receives over 19 million visitors from home and abroad each year.

_____

48. If you are interested and enthusiastic, fill in the electronic application form online.

49. Its aim is to thank volunteers around the world for giving their time and energy to help others and to encourage more people to do volunteer work.

50. What important news it is!

51. How time flies!

52. 学生们期待着做一些志愿者工作的机会。
The students _____ the opportunity to do some volunteer work.

53. 我写信来申请这个职位。
I'm writing to _____ the position.

54. 在这里，你可以交到新朋友。
You can _____ here.

55. 有些夫妇愿意生二胎。
Some couples _____ give birth to a second child.

56. 多么难忘的一段经历啊！

57. 迈克的爱好是集邮。

58. 我能教小孩子怎么保护海洋。

59. 我们会考虑你的申请，尽快通知你结果。

60. 他们是多么负责任的老师啊！

期中检测题

一、单项选择。（每小题1分，共15分）

1. His history is as _____ as his Chinese.
   A. good B. better C. the better D. best

2. _____ does your brother go back home? — Four times a month.
   A. How long B. What time C. How often D. How many

3. _____ interesting book!
   A. What B. What an C. What a D. How an

4. I'll never forget the day _____ I came to Qingdao for the first time.
   A. that B. when C. which D. in which

5. I _____ to bed until I finished my homework.
   A. went B. would go C. didn't go D. won't go

6. He didn't tell us _____ .
   A. where does she live B. where she lives
   C. where did she live D. where she lived

7. — Will you go to the museum with me this afternoon?
   — _____ . My aunt is coming to see me.
   A. Congratulations B. No problem
   C. Sorry, I can't D. Glad to hear that

8. — What time is the flight to Beijing on Saturday?
   — Wait a minute. Let me _____ in the schedule.
   A. look at it B. look for it C. look after it D. look it up

9. In _____ 1980's, most people in China went to work by _____ bike.
   A. the; a B. the; the C. the; / D. a; /

10. Nick _____ be at home now, for I saw him leave his house just now.
    A. must B. mustn't C. can D. can't

11. Jack was killed _____ the early morning of 1 May, 1945.
    A. in B. at C. on D. for

12. She _____ for her mother at 8 yesterday morning.
    A. is waiting B. waited C. was waiting D. waiting

13. She gets up early _____ catch the bus.
    A. so that B. in order to C. that D. so

14. Please don't forget _____ the lights before you leave.
    A. to turn off B. turning off C. to turn on D. turning on

15. — When _____ the hospital _____ ?
    — Next year.
    A. will; be built B. will; build
    C. was; built D. is; built

二、语言运用。（每小题1.5分，共15分）

Part A

16. The sign shows that you can't use _____ .
    A. cameras B. computers C. mobile phones

17. Can you tell us what time it is?
    A. It's forty-five to eleven. B. It's a quarter to eleven.

C. It's a quarter past eleven.

18. How many kinds of pollution are mentioned according to the chart?

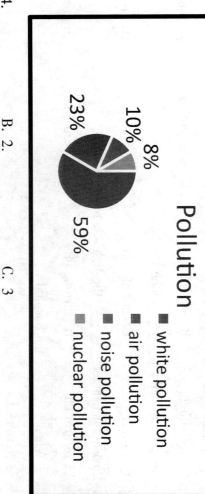

A. 4.   B. 2.   C. 3

19. When you see the picture, you should drive _____.

A. less than 65 km/h   B. more than 60 km/h
C. more than 65 km/h

20. When you see the sign, you can _____.

A. turn left   B. turn right   C. go straight

21. When we _____ we often see this sign.

A. can dive   B. can't dive   C. can't swim

22. The sign tells us that we _____ here.

A. jog   B. drive   C. walk

Part B

23. The flight number is _____.
A. VIE   B. DJ639   C. PEK

24. The passenger took _____ piece(s) of baggage (行李).
A. 1   B. 3   C. 2

25. The flight took _____ to arrive at the destination (目的地).

A. 9hr35m   B. 13hr35m   C. 14hr25m

三、阅读理解。(每小题2分，共40分)

A

Babysitter(临时保姆) needed	**Rose Hotel part-time work**
We need a babysitter to look after our two boys aged 5 and 7 after school from 4:30 p.m. to 6:30 p.m., Monday to Friday. $100 a week. Call Vicky at 6783-4521	We are lookinbg for part-time workers to work in our hotel on Saturdays. Come in (8 a.m. to 6 p.m.) or call Mina at 6123-8745(after 6 p.m.)
Holiday job	**Newspaper delivery(递送)**
Do you want to make some money this summer? Can you speak another language? We need French, Spanish or German speakers to work in the City Museum shop from Tuesday to Saturday. Send your CV(简历) to citymuseum@shopjob.lk.	We need young people to deliver newspaper on Monday, Wednesday and Friday mornings. The newspaper delivery takes 30 minutes in the village of Clanbrook. You must deliver the newspapers before 7:30 a.m., and you must have your own bike. Interested? Ask for more information at Clanbrook post office.

26. How much can a babysitter get for an hour?
  A. 5 dollars.   B. 7 dollars.   C. 10 dollars.   D. 12 dollars.
27. If Joy wants to get the job in Rose Hotel, she can call Mina at _____.
  A. 8 a.m.   B. 10 a.m.   C. 5 p.m.   D. 7 p.m.
28. What can we know about the holiday job?
  A. It doesn't require any CV.
  B. It doesn't provide any pay.
  C. If you have got it, you needn't work on Monday.
  D. If you want to get it, you must speak three languages.
29. If Harry takes the newspaper delivery job, he must _____.
  A. work three mornings a week   B. use the bike of the post office
  C. finish the work before 7:00 a.m.   D. be interested in the newspaper
30. The four pieces of information above may be found in the part of _____ in a newspaper.
  A. News   B. Ad(广告)
  C. Sports   D. Recreation(娱乐)

B

STUDY HELP

For many tests and exams, you are tested on your abilities to communicate successfully. In order to speak English fluently, you need to think in English. If you don't, your speech will be slow and it won't sound natural. Here are some things you can do to practice thinking in Englishl.

• Look at objects around your home and school, and think of what they are called in English. Try to make a direct connection between the object and the English word.
• When you are out in a public place, practice describing the things and people you see in your mind. For example, think, "There is a man walking down the street. He's wearing a suit. I think he is going to work." Try to think in English first, not in your first language.
• When you have to say something in English, think first and ask yourself, "What words and phrases do I know in English that I can use in this situation?" Try not think in your first language and translate your ideas into English. If you do, you will get frustrated very quickly.

Try these tips and you'll soon find that you are thinking in English.

31. The passage is most probably written to _____.
  A. students   B. teachers   C. parents   D. reporters
32. The writer gives us some advice on how to _____.
  A. greet people in English   B. practice thinking in English
  C. write an article in English   D. improve English listening skills
33. The passage above might be from the _____ column in a magazine.
  A. News Corner   B. Story Garden
  C. Language World   D. Technology Square

C

Jack, a 36-year-old man in Australia's northern city Darwin, was praised on Thursday for jumping onto a crocodile's back to save his wife Wendy at National Park, a local newspaper reported.

Wendy was standing on a river bank when the saltwater crocodile lunged, locking its jaws on both her legs as it tried to drag her underwater. Jack, who with his wife had been collecting water, immediately went to help her. He jumped onto the back, poked the eyes of the crocodile and finally got his wife free.

Wendy was later taken to Royal Hospital for a medical treatment. The doctors said she was suffering eight puncture wounds in her right leg, a puncture wound in her left leg and a serious cut to one of her fingers. "This could have been a fatal and tragic situation," said the general manager of Royal Hospital. Dr Leon, according to a local report. He said Wendy was saved by her husband's "quick and diligent actions".

34. This passage is most likely to be found in _____.
A. a travel guide   B. a newspaper   C. a textbook   D. a novel

35. The crocodile attacked Wendy when she was _____.
A. swimming in the river   B. standing on the river bank
C. watching the crocodile   D. fishing in the water

36. Which of the following statements is TRUE about Jack's wife?
A. Her eyes were badly poked.
B. She had eight wounds altogether.
C. One of her fingers also got hurt.
D. One of the crocodile's teeth was found in her leg.

37. Which of the following would be the best title for this passage?
A. The Husband Should Save the Wife.
B. A Man Saves Wife's Life From Crocodile's Jaws.
C. A Crocodile is Not So Dangerous as People Imagine.
D. Human Beings can Beat Crocodiles Sometimes.

D

There are many ways to find a job. It can be as easy as walking into a neighborhood store to look at its announcement board. Local stores often have areas where people can put small signs telling what kind of service they need or can provide. Such services include caring for children or cleaning houses.

Or, job searchers can look in the newspaper. Local newspapers have employment announcements placed by companies seeking workers.

Another popular tool for finding jobs is the Internet. For example, people in four hundred and fifty cities around the world can use the Craigslist Web site to buy objects, meet people or find a job.

Another useful way to find a job is through a college or university. For example, students at the University of Texas in Austin can go to the Career Exploration Center to get help in finding a job.

Some experts also help people find jobs. Susan W. Miller owns a company called California Career Services in Los Angeles. She says her company helps people find jobs by first helping them understand their strengths, goals and interests. Then she provides them with methods and resources to help them find the right job.

38. What is the passage mainly about?
A. Finding a job.   B. College students' part-time jobs.
C. Craigslist Web site.   D. The relation between study and work.

39. How many ways of finding a job are mentioned in the passage?
A. Three.   B. Four.   C. Five.   D. Six.

40. Which is NOT true according to the passage?
A. Local newspapers haven't employment announcements.
B. Some experts can help people find jobs.
C. People can find a job through internet.
D. There are many ways to find a job.

E

Mr. Lee was in bed and was trying to go to sleep when he heard the bell ring. He turned on the light and looked at his clock. It was twelve o'clock. "Who can it be at this time of night?" He thought. He decided to go and find out. So he got of bed, put on his dressing gown and went to the door. When he opened the door, there was nobody there. "That is very strange." Then he went back to his bedroom, took off his dressing gown, got back into bed, turned off the light and tried to go to sleep.

A few minutes later he heard the bell again. Mr. Lee jumped out of bed very quickly and rushed to the door. He opened it, but again he found no one there. He closed the door and tried not to feel angry. Then he saw a piece of paper on the floor. He picked it up. There were some words on it: "It is now after midnight, so it is April Fool's Day. April fool to you!"

"Oh, it was the English boy next door!" Mr. Lee exclaimed and almost smiled. He went back to bed and fell asleep at once. The bell did not ring again.

41. The bell rang _____ times in this passage.
    A. 1   B. 2   C. 3   D. 4

42. When did Mr. Lee go to bed?
    A. Before twelve o'clock.   B. After twelve o'clock.
    C. When the bell rang.   D. When he saw the boy.

43. Why did he rush to the door when he heard the bell ring the second time?
    A. He wanted to open the door for the visitor.
    B. He wanted to find out who the visitor was.
    C. He was afraid of the ring.
    D. He was waiting for someone.

44. From this passage, we learn that we can _____ on April Fool's Day.
    A. say "Hello" to each other   B. dance and sing at night
    C. play jokes on each other   D. send presents to children

45. Mr. Lee thought the boy _____.
    A. was a bad boy   B. was friendly with him
    C. shouldn't ring the bell at midnight   D. did a dangerous thing just now

四、补全对话。(每小题1分，共5分)

A: We have to meet the others at 8:30 at the reserve, don't we?
B: 46_____
A: Do you know how to get there?
B: 47_____ It will take us about two hours to get there by bus.
A: 48_____
B: It's an area that protects lots of different animals.
A: 49_____
B: I'm not really sure. I know there are many different kinds of birds there and I'm going to take my camera with me.
A: 50_____ What clothes are you going to wear?
B: Well, if it's wet, I will wear my strong shoes and take my raincoat with me.
A: So will I.

A. Nice to meet you.
B. That's a good idea.
C. What kinds of animals shall we see there?
D. Neither will I.
E. Yes, I've got a map.
F. What do you know about it?
G. Yes, that's right.

五、英汉互译。(每小题2分，共10分)

51. We may get on well with a number of people.

52. I was very glad to hear this because I was looking forward to seeing my grandpa.

53. In fact, smoking is bad for people's health.

54. 如果我们充分利用现在生活中常用的购物方式，并简单表达自己的观点(100词左右)。
If we _____ TV and the Internet, we will learn a lot from them.

55. 我将不会放弃学习英语。
I will never _____ English.

六、书面表达。(共15分)

网上购物是我们现在生活中常用的购物方式，请根据以下要点写一篇关于网上购物利弊的短文，并简单表达自己的观点(100词左右)。

利：1. 网店仅给出商品的图片；
    2. 24 小时营业，随时可购物；
    3. 便宜。

弊：1. 网店仅给出商品的图片；
    2. 不能检查质量；
    3. 不能享受和朋友一起购物的乐趣。

Unit 5 单元测试

一、根据首字母或中文意思完成句子。(5小题，每题1分)

1. His voice is more a_____ than his appearance.
2. I am not familiar with his c_____.
3. The e_____ has attracted thousands of visitors.
4. I was very i_____ by his story.
5. With the development of science and t_____, people's life becomes more and more convenient.

二、从方框中选择正确的短语并用正确的形式填空。(5小题，每题2分)

| as early as   search for   date back to   be influenced by   prepared for |

6. She worked hard _____ the interview.
7. The temple is believed to _____ the 15th century.
8. _____ 6 o'clock in the morning, I started to get up.
9. I _____ a place to eat, but couldn't find a good one.
10. Mike _____ deeply _____ his father.

三、单项选择。(10小题，每题1分)

11. This is exactly _____ house I am looking for.
    A. a   B. an   C. the   D. /
12. It is necessary _____ us to learn a foreign language.
    A. in   B. of   C. to   D. for
13. _____ do you like your fish cooked? Well-done or medium?
    A. When   B. Who   C. How   D. What
14. Tom is looking forward to _____ a chance to visit the modern China.
    A. having   B. have   C. has   D. had
15. You are my best friend. I never suspect _____ you say.
    A. what   B. that   C. why   D. how
16. I really don't know _____ he is talking about.
    A. that   B. when   C. how   D. what
17. Most young people find _____ exciting to watch a football match.
    A. it   B. this   C. that   D. one
18. The woman asked the policeman where _____.
    A. the post office is   B. the post office was
    C. is the post office   D. was the post office
19. Do you know if _____ back next week? If he _____ back, please let me know.
    A. he comes; will come   B. will he come; comes
    C. he will come; comes   D. will he come; will come
20. — Coffee or tea, sir? — _____
    A. Go ahead.   B. You are welcome.
    C. Coffee, please.   D. None of your business.

四、语言应用。(5小题，每题2分)

21. The sign is most likely to warn _____.
    A. drivers   B. children   C. runners
22. You can't _____ when you see the sign.
23. What time is it most likely to be now?
    A. drive too fast   B. drive slowly   C. turn right

A. 10:55.	B. 11:18.	C. 11:33.

24. You can get the shoes for _____.

A. $150	B. $175	C. $350

25. Where can we see this sign? In a _____.

```
X-Ray →
Radiology → Prenatal
          → Occupational
            Therapy
          ← Elevators
```

A. middle school	B. hospital	C. cinema

五、阅读理解。(15 小题，每题 2 分)

A

One day, a poor farmer was taking a bag of rice to the town. Suddenly the bag fell down from his horse on the road. He didn't know what to do about it because it was too heavy for him to lift (举起) it by himself. He only hoped that somebody would soon pass (经过) by and help him. Just at this moment a man riding a horse came up to him. But the farmer was very <u>disappointed</u> when he saw who he was. It was the great man living nearby. The farmer had hoped to ask another farmer or a poor man like him for help.

But surprisingly, the great man got off his horse as soon as he came near. He said to the farmer, "I see you need help, my friend. How good it is that I'm here just at the right time!" Then he took one end of the bag, the farmer took the other. They together lifted it and put it on the horse.

"Sir," asked the farmer, "how can I pay you?"

"It's quite easy," the great man answered with a smile, "Wherever you see anyone in trouble, do the same for him."

26. What happened when the farmer went to town?
A. His horse's leg was hurt.	B. The bag fell down from his horse.
C. The farmer lost his bag.	D. His bag was stolen.

27. The farmer didn't lift the bag onto the horse by himself because _____.
A. the bag was broken	B. the horse went away
C. the bag was too heavy	D. the farmer was ill

28. What does the underlined word "disappointed" mean?
A. Happy.	B. Feel down.
C. Excited.	D. Surprised.

29. What do you think of the great man?
A. He is mean about money.	B. He isn't a great man.
C. He isn't popular with others.	D. He is really a great man.

30. What does the story mainly tell us?
A. Everyone should become a great man.
B. Everyone should help the man who is in trouble.
C. Everyone should pay for other's help.
D. Everyone couldn't learn from the farmer.

B

When Mencius(孟子) was a small boy, his father died. So Mencius and his mother were quite poor.

One day, Mencius returned home from school and found his mother making some cloth. It was very beautiful and expensive.

"How much of your book have you read today?" Mencius' mother asked him. Mencius threw down his book. "I haven't read any of it." He replied, "I played with some friends of mine in the fields."

When his mother heard this, she picked up a pair of scissors(剪刀) and cut the cloth. "Why have you cut your cloth?" Mencius asked, "It was so beautiful and now you've wasted it." "You have wasted your time," she said, "Now I have wasted mine. Look at the terrible thing we have done!"

Mencius learned a lot from this lesson. After this, he always studied hard.

31. When did the story happen?
A. When Mencius was 30 years old.   B. When Mencius was a small boy.
C. When Mencius father lived with them.   D. When Mencius family was very rich.

32. The phrase "make some cloth" means "_____".
A. 织布   B. 做衣服   C. 纺棉花   D. 缝衣服

33. Why did Mencius' mother cut the cloth? Because _____.
A. she wanted to give her son a lesson
B. she thought it was wasting time to make cloth
C. she wanted to let her son get angry
D. she wanted to make some more beautiful cloth

34. Why did Mencius always study hard after this? Because _____.
A. he wanted to be a teacher   B. he wanted to make his mother happy
C. he learned a lot from the lesson   D. he didn't play with any other friends

35. This passage mainly tells _____.
A. a story about Mencius wasting time   B. a story of Mencius' mother
C. a story of Mencius and his friends   D. Mencius' mother cut the cloth

C

As the saying goes, "A hero is known in the time of misfortune(不幸)". Zhong Nanshan is a hero like this. He is a doctor in Guangdong, who saved many people's lives in 2003.

In 2003, SARS("非典") broke out (爆发) in Guangdong. Later, it spread (传播) across China and other parts of the world. Hundreds of patients even died from the disease. Patients coughed a lot and got fevers. Even many doctors and nurses got SARS when they treated patients. So everyone was afraid of it. But Zhong was brave enough to fight the disease. Zhong spent days and nights finding the cause of the disease. And with his way of treating, many patients began to get better. Zhong finally won people's trust.

In early 2020, a disease called Novel Coronavirus pneumonia(新型冠状病毒) hit Wuhan. It spread quickly-about tens of thousands of Chinese people were infected(感染). Zhong, 84, led his team to Wuhan to fight the illness. Zhong's team took many measures (措施) to cure the patients with Novel Coronavirus pneumonia. He advised people to wear masks, wash hands frequently(频繁地), stay at home and not to go to crowed places. Zhong likes sports very much. Although he was 67, he could still play basketball.

At the age of 85, Zhong still treats patients in the hospital and teaches young doctors. "I am just a doctor," Zhong says. But we think he is a hero and a fighter.

36. Where was the SARS broken out?
A. Guangdong.   B. Wuhan.   C. Shanghai.   D. Beijing.

37. How old does Zhong Nanshan still treat patients in the hospital?
A. 87.   B. 86.   C. 85.   D. 84.

38. Which one is TRUE according to the passage?
A. We can go to crowed places.
B. Zhong's team took many measures to cure the patients with Novel Coronavirus pneumonia.
C. Although he was 67, he could still play football.
D. In 2004, SARS broke out in Guangdong.

39. What's the main idea of the passage?
A. Doctors are the heroes.
B. Zhong is a hero and a fighter.
C. The difference between SARA and Novel Coronavirus pneumonia.
D. Novel Coronavirus pneumonia is very serious.

40. What's the meaning of "A hero is known in the time of misfortune(不幸)"?
A. 救死扶伤，大爱无疆。

六、把左右栏相对应的句子匹配起来。(5小题，每题1分)

41. I'm leaving for Canada on a study trip next week.   A. Really? It's very kind of you.
42. Do you think I can use your car for one day?   B. Enjoy your trip.
43. Lily, let me show you how to cook delicious food.   C. Not at all.
44. Jerry, do you mind my pointing out your mistake?   D. The same to you.
45. Wish you a happy New Year!   E. I am afraid not.

七、英汉互译。(15小题，每题2分)

46. we are all very interested in Ancient Greece.

47. They were attracted to each other from the first.

48. We were impressed by her enthusiasm.

49. The picture is a national treasure.

50. Paper-cut is one of the oldest forms of folk art in China.

51. 你听说过丝绸之路吗？
    Have you _____ _____ the Silk Road?

52. 我们住的房子不大不小。
    The house we live is _____ big _____ small.

53. 杰克被派到上海去出差一周。
    Jack _____ _____ Shanghai on business for a week.

54. 每天上午我要花半个小时练习瑜伽。
    It usually _____ me an hour _____ practice Yoga every morning.

55. 我们期待着再次见到您。
    We are _____ _____ seeing you again.

56. 古丝绸之路有着悠久的历史。

57. 张老师问我为什么总是上学迟到了？

58. 老师告诉她什么时候能来。

59. 他不知道太阳总是从东方升起来。

60. 甚至现在他的思想都在影响着我们。

B. 幸得有你，山河无恙。

C. 哪有什么岁月静好，只不过是一直有人替我们负重前行。

D. 时势造英雄。

Unit 6 单元测试

一、根据首字母或中文意思完成句子。(5小题，每题1分)

1. His laziness makes it impossible for him to a _____ success.
2. The carving is a superb piece of c _____.
3. This boy is very outgoing and c _____.
4. I'm ordinary yet u _____.
5. If she hadn't been so _____ (坚持不懈的), she might not have gotten the job.

二、从方框中选择正确的短语并用正确的形式填空。(5小题，每题2分)

| neither... nor... | focus on | take up | in the end | be connected to |

6. We shall _____ the needs of a customer.
7. _____ he _____ she will come to his party.
8. Mary's dream came true _____.
9. The keyboard _____ my computer.
10. He was eager to _____ some job.

三、单项选择。(10小题，每题1分)

11. The flowers will die unless they _____ every day.
    A. water   B. are watered
    C. watered   D. is watered

12. Xu Haifeng _____ as a national hero for winning the first Olympic gold medal for China in 1984.
    A. regard   B. has regarded
    C. was regarded   D. be regarded

13. It is said that another new car factory _____ next month.
    A. is building   B. will be built
    C. will built   D. is built

14. Waste paper shouldn't _____ everywhere. Its our duty to keep our school clean.
    A. are thrown   B. throw
    C. is thrown   D. be thrown

15. Jack _____ a job in a big company, but to our surprise, he didn't take it.
    A. is offered   B. was offered
    C. offered   D. has offered

16. I'll go abroad to study further if I _____ the job.
    A. am not offered   B. wasn't offered
    C. won't be offered D. am not to be offered

17. When water _____, it will be turned into vapor(蒸汽).
    A. is heated   B. heating
    C. are heated   D. heats

18. The car _____ in the traffic accident.
    A. destroyed   B. was destroyed
    C. destroys   D. has destroyed

19. — When _____ the hospital _____?
    — Next month.
    A. will; be built   B. was; built
    C. has; been built   D. is; built

20. I _____ to get to the airport before 7:00a.m. tomorrow. So I'll have to get up early.
    A. told   B. have told   C. was told   D. is told

四、语言应用。(5小题，每题2分)

21. Which of the following statements is right?

    A. It is a wedding invitation.
    B. It is a retiring invitation.
    C. It is a meeting invitation.

22. Which of the following statements is NOT right?

— 1 —

23. You can see the following sign in a _____.

A. Experience in CEO is needed.
B. If you want to be a sales manager, you can apply for the position.
C. If you want to work there, you should have a good knowledge of digital marketing strategy.

24. Where can you most probably see this?

A. sitting room   B. kitchen   C. public bathroom

25. What will happen according to the picture?.

A. In a library.   B. In a bookstore.   C. In a cinema.

五、阅读理解。(15 小题，每题 2 分)

A

A. They want to have a walk in the park.
B. They want to have a picnic in the park.
C. They want to see the animals in the park.

One of my favorite things to do in my free time is snow skiing, and as a middle-aged man, I have recently started snowboarding as well. Luckily, there are about five ski resorts near my hometown, so there are plenty of places to ski.

In order to ski, you need some basic equipment including snow skis, ski poles, ski boots, goggles, and some warm ski clothing. I bought my equipment last year after the season was over when everything was on sale.

When I go skiing, I load my skis on the top of my car and drive to the nearest ski resort. I usually buy a season ski pass that allows me to go skiing as often as I want. When I arrive at the ski resort, I put on my ski boots and skis and head directly for one of the ski lifts. The ski resort has a number of ski runs for beginning, intermediate, and expert skiers. Personally, I usually ski down intermediate runs that have a few moguls (鉴起点) to test my skills. I sometimes lose my balance or control and fall down on the runs, but that is part of the fun of skiing. I always have to be careful not to run into anyone as I go down the ski runs.

Recently, I've decided to take up snowboarding, but it's taking a little time to get the hang of it. Snowboarding is becoming more and more popular now that it is an Olympic event.

26. What does the author like to do in his spare time?

A. Visiting his hometown.   B. Watching the Olympics.

C. Car driving.	D. Snow skiing.

27. Why did the author buy his equipment after the season?
A. It was cheaper.	B. It was available then.
C. He had a season ski pass.	D. He wanted to improve his skills.

28. What can we learn about the author from Paragraph 3?
A. He finds fun challenging himself on skiing runs.
B. He usually runs to the ski resort in ski boots.
C. He always runs into someone when skiing.
D. He often chooses the runs for beginners.

29. What does the underlined phrase "get the hang of" in Paragraph 4 probably mean?
A. Watch.	B. Learn.
C. Run out of.	D. Catch up with.

30. Why do more and more people enjoy snowboarding?
A. It is much easier than snow skiing.
B. People have more free time nowadays.
C. It has become an event of the Olympics.
D. There are more resorts for snowboarding.

B

During a job interview, it's usual for the interviewers to ask about your weak points. For example, they might say "Tell me your three weakest points." or "What weak points do you think you have as a worker?". They want to see how you react, test how honest you are, and check if you have the ability to be true to yourself.

Avoid giving such answers as "I'm too organized", "I work too much", or "I'm too much of a perfectionist".

If they ask you about your weak points, answer honestly. Try not to turn them around and present them as strengths. If you do, the interviewers may think you're not telling the truth and are hiding your weak points.

Nobody's perfect. We all have flaws, areas in which we could improve. Try to answer the questions that the interviewers ask you instead of saying what you want them to hear.

Respond wisely. It means thinking before speaking. Don't rush when you talk about your weak points. Think for a little while before you share your observations (观察) and considerations. When you talk about your weak points, briefly explain when they tend to happen and what you're doing to improve them. This isn't an easy task because your weak points often form a pattern of behavior that's developed over time. Therefore, it also takes time to realize this and change it. But, you can show that you have realized these weak points and that you are trying to improve them.

31. Why do the interviewers often ask about your weak points?
A. To test your ability.	B. To check your honesty.
C. To show their care.	D. To express their eagerness.

32. What should you avoid when answering questions about your weak points?
A. Thinking before speaking.	B. Answering in an honest way.
C. Explaining when you have them.	D. Describing them as strong points.

33. What does the underlined word "flaws" in paragraph 4 probably mean?
A. Weaknesses.	B. Failures.
C. Difficulties.	D. Worries.

34. What's the purpose of the text?
A. To tell how to improve weak points.
B. To explain how to manage your time.
C. To offer some advice for an interview.
D. To discuss some skills to ask questions.

35. Where is the text most likely from?
A. A diary.	B. A novel.
C. A dictionary	D. A magazine.

C

Easier is better with the Jitterbug

The easy-to-use Jitterbug Flip has big buttons (按键) and a special Start button on the keyboard.

EASY TO USE: The large bright screen and simple YES and NO button make setting the menu simple. Plus, the powerful speaker ensure every talk will be loud and clear.

EASY TO ENJOY: Wherever you go, a built-in camera makes it easy to take photos and share your favorite memories. And with a long-lasting battery, you won't have to worry about remain lack of power.

EASY TO BE PREPARED: In any uncertain or unsafe situation, simply press the Start button and an agent will confirm your location, evaluate (评估) your situation and get you the help you need at any time.

The Jitterbug Flip is one of the most affordable cell phone on the market, with price as low as $14.99/month. For a limited time, get 25% off!

To order or learn more, call 1-800-358-3219, or visit us at Great Call com. Flip.

36. This passage is most likely _____.
   A. a notice   B. a poster
   C. an instruction   D. an advertisement

37. The Jitterbug Flip is a _____.
   A. phone   B. toy   C. speaker   D. camera

38. The Flip contains all of the following EXCEPT _____.
   A. a built-in camera   B. a powerful speaker
   C. a large touch screen   D. a long-lasting battery

39. If you need help while using Jitterbug Flip, the easiest way is to _____.
   A. cry for help   B. call 1-800-358-3219
   C. visit the company's website   D. press the "Start" button

40. Which of the following is mentioned about the Flip?
   A. It's color.   B. It's function.
   C. It's style.   D. It's weight.

六、把左右栏相对应的句子匹配起来。（5小题，每题1分）

41. Emergency Assistance, may I help you?   A. Yes, I got it just two weeks ago.
42. What is he interested in?   B. I'll take part in a social activity with my sister.
43. What's your plan for this summer holiday?   C. I've just been robbed.
44. Is it true that you have got a new job?   D. He is interested in fishing.
45. Would you want to see a film tonight?   E. Yes, I'd love to.

七、英汉互译。（15小题，每题2分）

46. 制表老师应该具备什么样的素质？

47. 对他们来说，什么是代代相传的。

48. 这些技艺在当时是代代相传的。

49. 我相信他的经验足以胜任这项工作。

50. 三思而后行。

51. 我想和负责人谈一谈。
I want to speak to the person _____.

52. 学校鼓励同学们参加一项自己喜欢的运动。
The school encourages students to _____ in a sport of their choice.

53. 看到他的发型时，我忍不住笑了。
I couldn't _____ when I saw his haircut.

54. 从前，河面上有一座石桥。
_____, there was a stone bridge over the river.

55. 我们将继续努力提高所有人的生活水平。
We will continue to _____ a better standard of living for all.

56. The label "made in China" can be seen everywhere.

57. Paper cutting is a traditional Chinese craft.

58. The rooms are cleaned every day.

59. The 2024 Olympics Games will be held in Paris.

60. All beginnings are hard.

Unit 7 单元测试

一、根据首字母或中文意思完成句子。(5 小题，每题 1 分)

1. The f_____ of the ear is to listen.
2. May I i_____ you to my uncle?
3. I p_____ staying at home to going out with them.
4. Rose was d_____ (怀疑) about the whole idea.
5. Cigarettes carry a health w_____ (警告).

二、从方框中选择正确的短语并用正确的形式填空。(5 小题，每题 1 分)

| in the beginning | turn off | be used for | online shopping | manage to |

6. Don't forget to _____ the lights when you leave the room.
7. _____, all things are hopeful.
8. We _____ get most of our produce in digital market.
9. It will _____ finding people in a fire or an earthquake.
10. _____ has had a big impact on traditional shopping malls.

三、单项选择。(10 小题，每题 1 分)

11. The team met a lot of difficulties, _____ they never gave up and won the game at last.
    A. and   B. but   C. or   D. so
12. Mike, don't be afraid to make mistakes, _____ you'll never make progress.
    A. and   B. but   C. or   D. so
13. Not only Mr. Smith but also Tom and Mary _____ late.
    A. was   B. is   C. were   D. be
14. Last night, I went to bed late, _____ I am really tired now.
    A. and   B. but   C. or   D. so
15. Hold your dream, _____ you're sure to succeed some day.
    A. and   B. but   C. or   D. so
16. Marie Curie didn't have much money when she was young, _____ she never stopped studying to be a scientist.
    A. although   B. because   C. so   D. but
17. I walked back _____ the others rode in the car.
    A. and   B. but   C. for   D. while
18. You'd better put on your sweater, _____ it's cold outside.
    A. and   B. but   C. for   D. while
19. —How do you like the book?
    —Very useful. Community safety is _____ introduced in it.
    A. specially   B. usually   C. badly   D. probably
20. It's hard _____ elderly people _____ the system.
    A. of; to operate   B. for; to operate
    C. of; operating   D. for; operating

四、语言应用。(5 小题，每题 2 分)

21. According to the picture, we stand _____ the yellow line.
    A. in front of   B. back from   C. on the right of

22. If you _____, you can go there.
    A. take a bus to the downtown   B. lose your way
    C. lose your suitcase

— 1 —

23. _____ Day falls on the April 1.

A. April's Fool   B. Children's   C. Mother's

24. According to the picture, we can touch someone to the heart by _____.

A. sending a gift   B. making a phone call
C. writing a letter

25. If you go to Gate 3, you should _____.

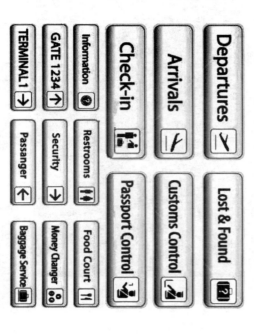

A. go straight   B. turn right   C. turn left

五、阅读理解。(15 小题，每题 2 分)

A

When your children do their homework, they may often meet some problems. How do children solve them? Some children choose to ask teacher for help. However, others choose to find out answers on the Internet.

Recently, an app called *zhuoyebang* is getting more and more popular. We can search for the answers of most of children's homework on it, and it often shows us the way of working out the questions. So many parents think it is useful for kids. In fact, most of the children choose to copy the answers to the questions directly instead of studying the process. It is convenient for them to finish homework. As a result, the children don't think it's necessary to listen to teachers carefully in classes. After a while, they find it difficult to follow their teacher in class.

Homework is useful to improve children's learning skills, but they are wasting time to do this kind of "homework".

What should parents do?

Let children know they must finish homework by themselves.

It is natural for a student to meet some problems when he or she is studying. They should think of it carefully instead of copying on the Internet.

As parents, you should take away the smart-phones from your children. Let children think by themselves.

26. This article is written for _____.

A. teacher   B. children   C. parents   D. the old

27. How do most of children solve the problems that they meet on *zhuoyebang*?

A. They ask teacher for help.
B. They think by themselves.
C. They discuss with their classmates.
D. They copy the answers to the questions directly.

28. Why do parents think the app is useful?

A. Because it shows how to work out the questions.
B. Because the children can copy the answers directly.
C. Because parents can learn a lot.
D. Because teachers can learn a lot.

29. How many suggestions does the writer give?

A. One.   B. Two.   C. Three.   D. Four.

30. Should children have smart-phones when they are learning?
   A. Yes, they should.   B. No, they shouldn't.
   C. It's hard to say.   D. Not mentioned.

B

After leaving school for many years, a group of students visited their teacher. All of them complained about problems and stress in their work and life.

The teacher went to the kitchen and returned with a large bottle of coffee and many kinds of cups—china, plastic and glass. He told them to help themselves to the coffee.

When all the students had a cup of coffee in their hands, the teacher said, "If you noticed, all the nice-looking and expensive cups had been taken, but the simple and cheap ones had been left behind. Although it is normal for you to want only the best for yourselves, that is the cause of your problems and stress. In fact, the cup itself adds no quality to the coffee. It is just a tool to hold what we drink."

What all of them really wanted was coffee, not the cups, but they all went for the best cups. And then they began to watch others' cups. Life is the coffee; jobs, money and the social position are the cups. The cups we have do not change the quality of our life. Sometimes, if we only pay attention to the cup, we will fail to enjoy the coffee.

The happiest people don't have the best of everything. They just make the best of everything.

31. According to the passage, the graduates were not satisfied because of _____.
   A. what the teacher did   B. the bad coffee
   C. the simple and cheap cups   D. their problems and stress

32. From the passage we can know that _____.
   A. the teacher gave out the cups to the graduates
   B. the teacher went to get the coffee and cups from the kitchen
   C. the teacher thought the jobs and money were more important
   D. the teacher had the best of everything

33. The teacher provided his students with many kinds of cups because _____.
   A. he wanted his students to enjoy the coffee
   B. he wanted to show his big collection of different kinds of cups
   C. he tried to tell the students how to understand life
   D. he hoped that they could have better cups

34. According to the passage, the teacher most probably agrees that _____.
   A. if you have all the best things for yourself, you will be happy
   B. the fewer complaints we have about life, the happier we will be
   C. we should work hard to get more money and higher social position to be happy
   D. a good life doesn't mean having more money, better jobs and higher social position

35. Which of the following is NOT TRUE according to the passage?
   A. No one chose the simple and cheap cups.
   B. It's normal for everyone to look forward to the best.
   C. We should pay more attention to the cups than the coffee.
   D. Try your best to make everything in your life best.

C

Computers are widely used in the world. As students, we can not only use them to relax, but also study online. Do you have any online classes? It is possible to take classes at home. All you need is a computer and an earphone.

However, most students don't seem to like online classes. Recently, over 2,000 students from 10 cities took part in a survey (调查). According to the survey, only about 35 percent of the students like taking such classes.

Many students said it was hard to focus on studying while taking online classes. This was true for Li Jing, 15, at No. 1 High School. "There are no classmates and no real teachers watching me. I can surf the Internet or do other things if I want to. It's harder to always stay focused," she said. Li Jing prepares a lot before taking her classes to make sure she will keep her attention. She also pushes herself to communicate with teachers. Students can come up with or answer questions while taking online classes.

Tian Lishan, 14, at No. 7 High School, thinks online interaction isn't enough. "The online teachers don't really get to know me. When I don't hand in homework, all I get is a short message instead of real **concern**," she said.

However, online classes still have advantages. "It saves time and money compared with taking offline classes. Also, if I don't understand some parts of a lesson, I can watch it over again," Li Jing said.

36. In the survey, about _____ students like taking online classes.
   A. 500   B. 600   C. 700   D. 2000

37. Taking online classes has the following advantages _____.
   ① save time ② hard to focus ③ enough interaction ④ save money
   ⑤ watch lessons over again
   A. ①②④   B. ②③⑤   C. ①③④   D. ①④⑤

— 3 —

38. The underlined word "concern" means "_____" in the passage.
    A. care   B. prize   C. promise   D. invitation
39. What can we learn according to the passage?
    A. Tian Lishan is a student from a high school in Beijing.
    B. Li Jing pushes herself to communicate with teachers in online classes.
    C. Li Jing thinks that online interaction isn't enough.
    D. Li Jing thinks it is easy to always stay focused.
40. The passage is mainly about _____.
    A. what the students think of online classes
    B. where the students take online class
    C. why the students like taking online classes
    D. how the students take online classes at home

六、把左右栏相对应的句子匹配起来。（5小题，每题1分）

41. What can I do for you?	A. So do I.
42. What's the function of it?	B. VR.
43. I like going shopping online.	C. I want to pick a drone.
44. What's your favorite digital products, Linda?	D. It's amazing.
45. How do you find 3D printer?	E. It can help with medical operations.

46. Believe it or not, technology has left a mark on our lives.
47. Technological innovations have truly changed our lives in so many ways.
48. There are all kinds of news and information on the Internet.
49. The Internet is an important means of communication.
50. It can help farmers check the growth of crops.
51. It's the latest product and is well received by customers.
52. 人们开始寻找进入太空的方法。

53. Man began _____ _____ ways to go into space.
54. 我们应该更好地利用网络，我们应该每天做运动。
    We should _____ better _____ Internet.
55. 在某种程度上这是个好消息。
56. That's good news _____ _____ _____.
57. 你能介绍一下你自己吗？
58. 比起夏天我更喜欢秋天。
59. 乘公交车去图书馆花了我一个小时。
60. 快一点，否则你会上学迟到。

— 4 —

Unit 8 单元测试

一、根据首字母或中文意思完成句子。（5小题，每题1分）

1. We should p_____ the Earth.
2. The number of some wild animals is d_____ (减少).
3. Can you give me more examples about _____ (可回收的) waste?
4. It was not until now that I r_____ (修复) the importance of protecting the environment.
5. The challenge now is to r_____ (修复) the home of the young fish.

二、从方框中选择正确的短语并用正确的形式填空。（5小题，每题2分）

| not until | dry up | global warming | garbage sorting | at the same time |

6. The river _____ because there is no water in the river.
7. It was _____ when they get to the school.
8. _____ the teacher came in did the students stop talking.
9. _____ is a good way to protect the environment.
10. _____ is becoming more and more serious.

三、单项选择。（10小题，每题1分）

11. It was last year _____ you taught me how to drive.
    A. when B. that C. where D. which
12. It was in the factory _____ produced TV sets _____ our friend was murdered.
    A. which; which B. that; which
    C. that; that D. where; that
13. — You are not so strong as he.
    — _____. However, he dosen't _____ me in intelligence.
    A. So I am; citizen B. So am I; comparison
    C. So I am; equal D. So am I; characteristic
14. It was _____ he said _____ disappointed me.
    A. that; what B. what; that C. what; what D. that; that
15. Ann is so careful that she always goes over her exercises to _____ there are no mistakes.
    A. look for B. make sure C. find out D. think about
16. — Which of the two English dictionaries will you buy?
    — I'll buy _____ of them, so I can give one to my friend, Hellen.
    A. either B. neither C. all D. both
17. He _____ two thousand trees since 1985.
    A. plants B. planted C. will plant D. has planted
18. — Dad, when will you be free? You agreed to go to the seaside with me four days ago.
    — I am sorry, Jean. But I think I will have a _____ holiday soon.
    A. four-days B. four-day C. four days D. four day
19. In the bookshop, a reader asked the shopkeeper _____ Who Moved My Cheese was an interesting book.
    A. that B. how C. what D. if
20. It was not until 1920 _____ regular radio broadcast began.
    A. while B. which C. that D. since

四、语言应用。（5小题，每题2分）

21. If the original price of a coat is 100 yuan, you only have to pay _____ yuan now.
    A. 130 yuan B. 70 yuan C. 30 yuan
22. If you see this sign in front of a house, it means that _____.
    A. there is a dog inside B. there is an alarm system
    C. there is a security camera D. that; that there are no

— 1 —

23. From the following sign we can know that _____ can park here.

A. privates cars　　B. taxis　　C. buses

24. The sign is usually seen in a shopping center and means _____.

A. the store is closed　　B. the store opens daily
C. the store will open soon

25. If you want to have your clothes dry-cleaned here, what do you have to do?

A. Have them dry-cleaned immediately.
B. Wait for some time.
C. Help repair the machine.

五、阅读理解。（15小题，每题2分）

A

Sleep is a very important part of our lives. After a long day, we all like the feeling of a soft bed. We know how good it will feel in the morning after we get some rest. Sleep is also very important to animals. They also need to sleep after they work hard.

Some animal sleep in the sea. Fish have no eyelids（眼睑）, so they sleep with their eyes open! Sea otters（海獭）sleep in seaweed（海草）on top of the sea. The seaweed keeps the otters from moving along. Most sharks（鲨鱼）keep swimming while they sleep. Some fish find a little hole in the coral（珊瑚）and hide so they can sleep.

Some animals sleep under the ground! When it's hot, many frogs sleep in a hole because they want to avoid the heat. Some frogs spend the whole summer in their holes. Groundhogs（土拨鼠）live in holes in the ground, so they also sleep underground.

What about animals that live above the ground? Birds sleep in their nests or on trees. A bird's claws（爪）close when they sleep. This helps them stay on the tree. Bats sleep upside down for twenty hours a day!

No matter what kind of animal you are, you need your sleep.

26. Why do fish sleep with their eyes open?
A. Because they must keep swimming.　　B. Because they have no eyelids.
C. Because they sleep in seaweed.　　D. Because they sleep in the coral.

27. Why do many frogs spend the summer in the holes?
A. To lay eggs.　　B. To get food.
C. To avoid the enemies.　　D. To avoid the heat.

28. How do bats sleep?
A. Upside down.　　B. In the hole.
C. On the tree.　　D. On its side.

29. What's the words "Bats" meaning?
A. 蝙蝠　　B. 猫头鹰　　C. 海鸥　　D. 燕子

30. The passage tells us that _____.
A. only people need sleep　　B. all animals need sleep
C. birds need sleep on the tree　　D. groundhogs sleep above the ground

B

It was a village in India. The people were poor. However, they were not unhappy. After all, their forefathers had lived in the same way for centuries.

Then one day, some visitors from the city arrived. They told the villagers there were some people elsewhere who liked to eat frog's legs. However, they did not have enough frogs of their own, and so they wanted to buy frogs from other places.

This seemed like money for nothing. There were millions of frogs in the fields around, and they were no use to the villagers. All they had to do was catch them. Agreement was reached, and the children were sent into the fields to catch frogs. Every week a truck arrived to collect the catch and hand over the money. For the first time, the people were able to dream of a better future. But the dream didn't last long.

The change was hardly noticed at first, but it seemed as if the crops were not doing so well. More worrying was that the children fell ill more often, and, there seemed to be more insects around lately.

The villagers decided that they couldn't just wait to see the crops failing and the children getting weak. They would have to use the money earned to buy pesticides (杀虫剂) and medicines. Soon there was no money left.

Then the people realized what was happening. It was the frog. They hadn't been useless. They had been doing an important job—eating insects. Now with so many frogs killed, the insects were increasing more rapidly. They were damaging the crops and spreading diseases.

Now, the people are still poor. But in the evenings they sit in the village square and listen to sounds of insects and frogs. These sounds of the night now have a much deeper meaning.

31. From Paragraph 1, we learn that the villagers _____.
    A. worked very hard for centuries
    B. dreamed of having a better life
    C. were poor but somewhat content
    D. lived a different life from their forefathers

32. Why did the villagers agree to sell frogs?
    A. The frogs were easy to earn money.
    B. They needed money to buy medicine.
    C. They wanted to please the visitors.
    D. The frogs made too much noise.

33. What might be the cause of the children's sickness?
    A. The crops didn't do well.
    B. There were too many insects.
    C. The visitors brought in diseases.
    D. The pesticides were overused.

34. What's the words "forefathers" meaning?
    A. 岳父   B. 祖父   C. 祖先   D. 祖母

35. What can we infer from the last sentence of the text?
    A. Happiness comes from peaceful life in the country.
    B. Health is more important than money.
    C. The harmony between man and nature is important.
    D. Good old days will never be forgotten.

C

We produce 500 billion of plastic bags in a year worldwide and they are thrown away polluting oceans, killing wildlife and getting dumped in landfills where they take up to 1,000 years to decompose. Researchers have been unsuccessfully looking for a solution.

The 16 year old Canadian high school student, Daniel Burd, from Waterloo Collegiate Institute, has discovered a way to make plastic bags degrade (分解) in as few as 3 months, a finding that won him first prize at the Canada-Wide Science Fair, a $10,000 prize, a $20,000 scholarship, and a chance to revolutionize a major environmental issue.

Burd's strategy was simple: Since plastic does eventually degrade, it must be eaten by microorganisms (微生物). If those microorganisms could be identified, we could put them to work eating the plastic much faster than under normal conditions.

With this goal in mind, he ground plastic bags into a powder and concocted (调制) a solution of household chemicals, yeast (酵母) and tap water to encourage microbes growth. Then he added the plastic powder and let the microbes work their magic for 3 months. Finally, he tested the resulting bacterial culture on plastic bags, exposing one plastic sample to dead bacteria as a control. Sure enough, the plastic exposed (暴露) to the live bacteria was 17% lighter than the control after six weeks.

The inputs are cheap: maintaining the required temperature takes little energy because microbes produce heat as they work, and the only outputs are water and tiny levels of carbon dioxide.

"Almost every week I have to do chores and when I open the closet door, I have piles of plastic bags falling on top of me. One day, I got tired of it and I wanted to know what other people are doing with these plastic bags. The answer: not much. So I decided to do something myself," said Daniel Burd.

36. Daniel Burd won first prize at the Canada-Wide Science Fair because _____.
    A. he found a new kind of microorganism
    B. he contributed much to environmental protection
    C. he found a way to degrade plastics in shorter time
    D. he could encourage microbes growth in an easier way

37. Daniel Burd exposed one plastic sample to dead bacteria to _____.
    A. make the live bacteria work better
    B. test how effective his method was

— 3 —

C. know which bacteria worked faster
D. control the temperature in the process

38. Maintaining the required temperature takes little energy because _____.
A. plastics can get hot easily
B. microbes can produce heat themselves
C. much carbon dioxide is produced
D. the temperature can be controlled

39. What's the words "Institute" meaning?
A. 机构. B. 组织. C. 学会. D. 俱乐部.

40. Daniel Burd got his idea from _____.
A. his school textbook   B. the failure of researchers
C. his everyday work   D. the practice of other people

六、把左栏相对应的句子匹配起来。（5小题，每题1分）

41. Today I read a book. This book about our environment is in danger. | A. People are killing more and more animals.
42. What air pollution people is making? | B. Yes, I read the book, too. Once our environment is very beautiful.
43. Should everyone protect the environment? | C. It is our duty to keep our environment clean and tidy. We can do a lot of things to protect our environment.
44. What is our duty? | D. Yes, everyone should make a contribution to protect the environment.
45. How to protect environment by ourselves? | E. Love flowers birds, protect birds, protect the animals. Save water, take good care of the resources.

七、英汉互译。（15小题，每题2分）

46. Planting trees are very helpful and important for us.

47. Protecting the environment is every man's responsibility.

48. The amount of water which is less and less.

49. No one can live without water or air.

50. If we don't save water, the last drop of water will be a tear-drop of us.

51. The protection of trees, that is, to protect themselves.

52. 他认出了她，可是假装没看到她。
Having recognized her, he _____ pretended not _____ to have seen her.

53. 正在修理的那台收音机是谁的？
_____ is the radio _____ repaired?

54. 正在翻译成英语的那本小说是一位青年作家写的。
The novel being _____ English was written by a young writer.

55. 我觉得有人溜进了我的房间。
I _____ somebody _____ my room.

56. 那孩子听到有人一步一步地在上楼梯。

57. 你每隔多久叫人把房间油漆一次？

58. 你的衣服是自己做的还是叫别人做的？

59. 关掉水龙头，别让水浪费掉。

60. 老师们不让孩子们在草地上玩。

期末检测题

第Ⅰ卷（共两部分：满分 70 分）

第一部分　英语知识运用。（共两节；满分 30 分）

第一节　单项选择。（共 15 小题；每小题 1 分，满分 15 分）

从 A、B、C、D 四个选项中，选出可以填入空白处的最佳选项，并在答题卡上将该项涂黑。

1. Sanya is _____ most beautiful sea city.
   A. /　　　　B. the　　　　C. a　　　　D. an

2. According to the timetable, the plane _____ off at 8:00 a.m.
   A. takes　　B. is going to take　　C. will take　　D. is taking

3. Sally really wants a cat, _____ her father won't let her have one.
   A. and　　　B. but　　　　C. so　　　　D. or

4. I am not sure _____ English is spoken in South Africa or not.
   A. weather　B. if　　　　C. that　　　D. whether

5. —_____ is he? — He is an engineer.
   A. Whose　　B. What　　　C. Who　　　D. Whom

6. —When did you buy the computer?
   —I have _____ this computer for 5 years, but it still works well.
   A. bought　　B. have　　　C. had　　　　D. had bough

7. I have told you about it many times and it was _____ of you to make the same mistake again.
   A. clever　　B. probable　　C. impossible　　D. stupid

8. —Do you mind my smoking here?
   —_____!
   A. No, thanks　　　　　　B. No, Good idea
   C. Yes. Better not　　　　D. Yes, please

9. There _____ some flowers on the teacher's desk just now, but now there _____ nothing on it.
   A. have; has　　B. were; was　　C. were; is　　D. has; has

10. It was in the library _____ I left my schoolbag yesterday afternoon.
    A. who　　　B. which　　　C. where　　　D. that

11. I love the weekend, because I _____ get up early on Saturdays and Sundays.
    A. needn't　　B. mustn't　　C. wouldn't　　D. shouldn't

12. _____, and you will see the house.
    —OK.
    A. If you stand　　　　　B. To stand
    C. When you stand　　　D. Stand

13. Do you know _____?
    A. where does she live　　B. she lives where
    C. where she lives　　　　D. where she lived

14. Many officers _____ to our school to exchange ideas about New Year's plans last week.
    A. was invited　　　　　B. were invited
    C. are invited　　　　　D. will invite

15. —We'll have the exam next week. I'm really worried.
    —_____.
    A. Just so so　　B. Take it easy　　C. No need　　D. Too early

第二节　语言应用。（共 10 小题；每小题 1.5 分，满分 15 分）

Part A

根据下列图片所提供的信息，从 16～22 题所给的 A、B、C 三个选项中，选出可以填入空白处的最佳选项，并在答题卡上将该项涂黑。

16. The sign tells us _____ in this area.
    A. if we will, we can swim　　B. we mustn't swim
    C. both fish and human beings can swim

17. We can get to 500 million friends by _____.

18. When you see the following sign, _____.

A. mail and twitter B. e-mail and book
C. facebook and tumblr

19. How can Jerry get to Watcz?

A. you can drive fast as soon as possible
B. you can't pass other cars
C. you must stop your car

20. The aim of this sign is to _____.

A. Turn right.   B. Turn left.   C. Go ahead.

21. From the picture, we know that there are many ways to _____ this box.

A. rent a house   B. sell a house   C. buy a house

22. You're advised _____.

A. do the bed   B. reuse   C. do arts

A. not to leave valuables in your car   B. to take good care of your car
C. to stay close to your car

Part B

根据下图提供的信息，从 23~25 题所给的 A、B、C 三个选项中，选出可以填入空白处的最佳选项，并在答题卡上将该项涂黑。

Snoopy World

Grown-up: $200

Child: $100

(over 10 persons—20% off)

Parking: car $50; motorcycle $20

Opening hours: 9:00 a.m.—6:00 p.m. (closed on Tuesday)

23. Mrs. Green visited the Snoopy World with her 2 children. She paid _____ for the tickets.
    A. $100   B. $200   C. $400

24. The Greens couldn't go there on _____.
    A. Tuesday   B. Thursday   C. 9:00 a.m.—6:00 p.m.

25. Mrs. Green drove her car to the Snoopy World. She should pay _____ for the parking.
    A. $100   B. $50   C. $20

第二部分 阅读理解。（五篇短文，共 20 小题；每小题 2 分，满分 40 分）

阅读下列短文，从每题所给的 A、B、C、D 四个选项中，选出最佳选项，并在答题卡上将该项涂黑。

A

I travel a lot, and I find out different "styles" of directions every time I ask "How can I get to the post office?"

Foreign tourists are often confused in Japan because most streets there don't have names; in Japan, people use landmarks(地标) in their directions instead of street names. For example, the Japanese will say to travelers, "Go straight down to the corner. Turn left at the big hotel and go past a fruit market. The post office is across from the bus stop."

In the countryside of the American Midwest, there are not usually many landmarks. There are no mountains, so the land is very flat; in many places there are no towns or buildings within miles. Instead of landmarks, people will tell you directions and distances. In Kansas or Iowa, for example, people will say, "Go north two miles. Turn east, and then go another mile."

People in Los Angeles, California, have no idea of distance on the map; they measure distance in time, not miles. "How far away is the post office?" you ask. "Oh," they answer "it's about five minutes from here." You say, "Yes, but how many miles away is it?" They don't know.

It's true that a person doesn't know the answer to your question sometimes. What happens in such a situation? A New Yorker might say, "Sorry, I have no idea." But in Yucatan, Mexico, no one answers "I don't know." People in Yucatan believe that "I don't know" is impolite. They usually give an answer, often a wrong one. A tourist can get very, very lost in Yucatan!

26. When a tourist asks the Japanese the way to a certain place, they usually _____.
    A. describe the place carefully
    B. show him a map of the place
    C. tell him the names of the streets
    D. refer to recognizable buildings and places

27. What is the place where people measure distance in time?
    A. New York.   B. Los Angeles.   C. Kansas.   D. Iowa.

28. What is the purpose of the author in writing this passage?
    A. To show cultural differences in showing directions.
    B. To show how to ask the way properly in different countries.
    C. To explain why people have similar understanding of direction.
    D. To share the experience of traveling around the world.

29. People in Yucatan may give a tourist a wrong answer _____.
    A. in order to save time   B. as a test
    C. so as to be polite   D. for fun

B

Some years ago, Chinese high school students would show their new schoolbags, new clothes or new pens to their classmates when the new term started. Today, however all have changed. If you still come back to school with only these things, you are falling out-of-date. Students in big cities like to bring the latest high-tech things to school, and feel happy and pleased to show off these things to others. Mobile phones, MP3 players, CD players, e-dictionaries, the list is <u>endless</u>.

Young people think that, living in the 21st century, they must keep up with the times. They don't want to fall behind. Besides, they think that they need to keep in touch with their classmates, so they need mobile phones. They also like to listen to pop music, so they need CD players. They explain that just like e-dictionaries, these can be useful in their study, too. They think that their parents should understand why they want these things.

Foreign students will also bring some latest high-tech things when they return to school at the beginning of a new term. So, they often use the money they made by themselves during the holiday to buy these high-tech things that they want.

30. Today if a student shows his new schoolbag to his classmates, he will probably _____.
  A. be laughed at   B. be encouraged
  C. be praised   D. be followed

31. The underlined word "endless" probably means _____.
  A. important in meaning   B. great in use
  C. small in size   D. large in number

32. What do Chinese young people think of the hi-tech things?
  A. They are expensive, but they're very useful.
  B. They're useful both in their lives and studies.
  C. They show a new beginning of their lives in a new term.
  D. They can help them catch up with others in study.

33. From the passage, we can know that _____.
  A. foreign students spend more money on high-tech things
  B. few foreign students ask their parents to buy high-tech things
  C. foreign students are more interested in high-tech things
  D. foreign students are less interested in high-tech things

C

An eight-year-old child heard her parents talking about her little brother. All she knew was that he was very sick and they had no money. Only a very expensive operation could save him now and there was no one to lend them the money.

When she heard her daddy say to her tearful mother, "Only a miracle can save him now," the little girl went to her bedroom and pulled her money from its hiding place and counted it carefully.

She hurried to a drugstore(药店) with the money in her hand.

"And what do you want?" asked the salesman. "It's for my little brother," the girl answered. "He's really, really sick and I want to buy a miracle." "Pardon?" said the salesman.

"My brother Andrew has something bad growing inside his head and my daddy says only a miracle can save him. So how much does a miracle cost?" "We don't sell a miracle here, child. I'm sorry," the salesman said with a smile.

"Listen, if it isn't enough, I can try and get some more. Just tell me how much it costs."

A well-dressed man heard it and asked, "What kind of a miracle does your brother need?"

"I don't know," she answered with her eyes full of tears. "He's really sick and mum says he needs an operation. But my daddy can't pay for it, so I have brought all my money."

"How much do you have?" asked the man. "$1.11, but I can try and get some more," she answered, "Well, what luck," smiled the man. "$1.11, the price of a miracle for little brothers."

He took up the girl's hand and said, "Take me to where you live. I want to see your brother and meet your parents. Let's see if I have the kind of miracle you need."

That well-dressed man was Dr. Carlton Armstrong, a famous doctor. The operation was successful and it wasn't long before Andrew was home again.

How much did the miracle cost?

34. In the eye of the little girl, a miracle might be _____.
  A. some wonderful medicine   B. something beautiful
  C. something interesting   D. some good food

35. The little girl said again and again "… I can try and get some more." That shows _____.
  A. she had still kept some money
  B. she thought money was easy to get
  C. there was no need to worry about money
  D. she hoped not to be refused

36. What made the miracle happen?
  A. The medicine from the drugstore.   B. The girl's money.
  C. The girl's love for her brother.   D. Nobody can tell.

37. From the passage we can infer(推断) that _____.
  A. the doctor didn't ask for any pay
  B. the little girl is lovely but not so clever
  C. a miracle can happen if you keep on
  D. andrew was in fact not so sick as they had thought

foreigners like a dish with chicken and cucumbers, which is called Gongbao Jiding.

Hop pot is a delicious meal that is uncommon in the West. There are tasty peanut sauces and different meats and vegetables. And you can eat as long as you like.

The first word that many foreigners learn in China is "beer". They use this word a lot. While they are drinking it, they love the different cooked meats on sticks, called chuan(串).

However, most Westerners come to China because it is different from home. They are open to eating something new. So don't be afraid to order your favorite dishes for them to have a try.

42. How does the Chinese dishes foreigners like taste?
   A. Sweet and sour.　　　　　　　　B. Hot and salty.
   C. Hot and sour.　　　　　　　　　D. Sweet and salty.

43. What is perhaps the first Chinese word lots of foreigners learn in China?
   A. 火锅　　　B. 烧烤　　　C. 鸡丁　　　D. 啤酒

44. The writer's advice to Chinese is _____.
   A. never order dishes for your foreign friends before you ask them
   B. feeling free to order what you like best for your foreign friends
   C. ordering western Chinese dishes for your foreign friends
   D. never order real Chinese dishes for your foreign friends

45. The best title of this passage is _____.
   A. Hot pot, a must dish for foreigners
   B. Tips on ordering dishes for foreigners
   C. Opening up the world of Chinese food
   D. Menus of real Chinese food

D

Channel 1(一频道)	Channel 2
18:00 Around China	17:45 Computers today
18:30 Children's programme(节目)	18:10 Foreign arts
19:00 News	18:30 Modern English
19:30 Weather report	19:00 Animal world
19:40 Around the world	19:25 In Asia
20:10 TV play: Sisters	20:20 Sports
21:00 English for today	21:00 Sports player: Yao Ming
21:15 Pop music	21:45 English news
21:55 Talk show	22:05 On TV next week

38. If you want to know something about Yao Ming, the best programme for you is _____.
   A. Talk Show　　B. Sports　　C. Sports player　　D. TV play

39. You'll know something about _____ at 19:00 on Channel 2.
   A. animals　　B. news　　C. foreign　　D. Asia

40. If you want to watch NBA, the best programme for you would be _____.
   A. foreign arts　　　　　　B. around the world
   C. sports　　　　　　　　　D. English news

41. If you like music very much, the best programme for you is _____.
   A. at 21:45 on Channel 2　　　　B. at 21:55 on Channel 1
   C. at 21:00 on Channel 2　　　　D. at 21:15 on Channel 1

E

I am hungry. I walk into a Chinese restaurant and sit down to order(点菜). I am confident. I have eaten Chinese food many times in America. I know what I like. I look at the picture menu and I'm shocked. Real Chinese food is very different from Western food.

And I am not alone. Many Westerners are surprised the first time they order food in China. It is different. It is also delicious.

My Chinese friends usually order certain dishes they know foreigners like. Westerners like sweeter foods, so sweet and sour pork is very popular. Everyone, even waiters, knows that

第Ⅱ卷(共三节；满分 30 分)

注意事项：

1. 必须使用 0.5 毫米黑色墨迹签字笔在答题卡上题目所指示的答题区域内作答。答在试题卷上无效。

2. 第Ⅱ卷共三节，满分 30 分。

第一节　补全对话。(共 5 小题；每小题 1 分，满分 5 分)

阅读下列对话，从所给选项中，选出能够完成对话的最佳选项，并将选项的字母代号写在答题卡相应的横线上。选项中有两个多余选项。

— 5 —

A: You are late today! You made me stand here for forty minutes.
B: I'm really sorry.
A: Why didn't you drive your car? 46
B: 47
A: Really? Are you going to live without a car?
B: I think our city is badly polluted because of the heavy traffic, and I have to spend lots of time sitting in the car.
A: 48
B: I am going to buy a bike and then ride to work.
A: 49
B: You're living a low-carbon life and it's also a good way to take exercise.
A: Good idea. 50

A. What made you do that?
B. But how are you going to work?
C. No, I am not.
D. When do you want to buy a new one?
E. Where do you usually park your car?
F. I have sold my car.
G. I had to wait for a bus a long time.

第二节 翻译。（共 5 小题；每小题 2 分，满分 10 分）

Part A 请将下面的英语句子翻译成汉语，并将答案写在答题卡相应的横线上

51. Don't judge a book by its cover.

52. The boy holding a football is my younger brother.

53. I prefer taking a bus or subway to taking a taxi.

Part B 请根据所给中文提示，将下列译成英语的句子补充完整，并把答案写在相应的横线上。

54. 在中国很多父母对其孩子要求很严格，尤其是作业。
In China, many parents _____ _____ _____ their children, especially about their homework.

55. 现在是高峰期，出租车可能会花很长时间。
It's _____ now. A taxi may take too long.

第三节 书面表达。（满分 15 分）

好心情可以使我们感到愉快、幸福，但是怎样才能保持一个好心情呢？请根据以下提示，以"How to Keep a Good Mood?"为题，用英语写一篇短文。

要点如下：(1)保持健康；(2)好好休息；(3)回忆过去自己高兴的事情；(4)多考虑事情的积极方面。

注意：(1)词数 80～100 词；(2)可适当增加细节，以使行文连贯。

单词提示：回忆 recall；积极方面 the positive aspect

参考答案

Unit 1 单元测试

一、根据首字母或中文意思完成句子。(5小题，每题1分)

1. (e)xperience   2. (p)roduct   3. unique   4. (r)eservation   5. (d)iscovered

二、从方框中选择正确的短语并用正确的形式填空。(5小题，每题2分)

6. pass through   7. set off   8. all sorts of   9. due to   10. scenic spot

三、单项选择。(10小题，每题1分)

11-15 BCDBA   16-20 AACAA

四、语言应用。(5小题，每题2分)

21-25 CBCBC

五、阅读理解。(15小题，每题2分)

26-30 BADCB   31-35 DDCBD   36-40 DACCB

六、把左右栏相对应的句子匹配起来。(5小题，每题1分)

41-45 CABED

七、英汉互译。(15小题，每题2分)

46. 这个男孩正在上部网上搜索当地的景点。
47. 山的上部终年被雪覆盖了。
48. 我迫不及待要去大寨沟游玩了。
49. 她热爱自由，希望探索大自然。
50. 我可以用信用卡在自动售票机上买票吗？
51. 17岁时，马可波罗开始了他的第一次旅行。
52. spent; travelling
53. worth visiting
54. takes; to
55. looking forward to
56. I'm interested in China and Chinese food.
57. Could you tell me more about this city?
58. Would you like to join us?
59. We often went to school by bus last year.
60. You should make a travel plan first.

Unit 2 单元测试

一、根据首字母或中文意思完成句子。(5小题，每题1分)

1. (a)ppointment   2. (s)tress   3. (t)emperature   4. reduce   5. energy

二、从方框中选择正确的短语并用正确的形式填空。(5小题，每题1分)

6. as a result   7. suffer from   8. lost his temper   9. burn off   10. will give you a hand

三、单项选择。(10小题，每题1分)

11-15 DBCBA   16-20 CDCAB

四、语言应用。(5小题，每题2分)

21-25 AACCA

五、阅读理解。(15小题，每题2分)

26-30 ACCAA   31-35 BBCDA   36-40 BCADA

六、把左右栏相对应的句子匹配起来。(5小题，每题1分)

41-45 CABED

七、英汉互译。(15小题，每题2分)

46. 我的家乡以优美的景色和美味的食物而著名。
47. 不鸣则已，一鸣惊人。
48. 如果你想亲近大自然，就一定会爱上云南。
49. 我喉咙痛和咳嗽得厉害。
50. 你应该避免油腻的食物。
51. 锻炼能降低人们受压力和抑郁的风险。
52. recover from
53. pay attention to

Unit 3 单元测试

一、根据首字母或中文意思完成句子。(5小题,每题1分)
1. (a)ssistant 2. (c)olleagues 3. (m)entor 4. (s)cholarship 5. (c)hallenge

二、从方框中选择正确的短语并用正确的形式填空。(5小题,每题2分)
6. deal with 7. were absent from 8. instead of 9. keep track of 10. go through

三、单项选择。(10小题,每题1分)
11-15 ABCBD 16-20 ACCDD

四、语言应用。(5小题,每题2分)
21-25 BCCCC

五、阅读理解。(15小题,每题2分)
26-30 BDBCB 31-35 BBCCA 36-40 CABCB

六、把左右栏相对应的句子匹配起来。(5小题,每题1分)
41-45 BDACE

七、英汉互译。(15小题,每题2分)
46. 我在打扫家里卫生时,突然有人敲我的门。
47. 不要班门弄斧。
48. 虽然阳光普照,但天气不暖和。
49. 我的妹妹正在看电视。
50. 汤姆过马路时,被卡车撞了。
51. 因为约翰经常来公司,所以助理接待员认识他。
54. make an appointment
55. look well
56. It's well known that good health is more important than wealth.
57. Be careful when you go across the road.
58. The bed is big enough for him.
59. It is necessary for you to have a walk.
60. He often gets into trouble.

Unit 4 单元测试

一、根据首字母或中文意思完成句子。(5小题,每题1分)
1. (a)pplication 2. (e)nthusiastic 3. (k)nowledge 4. responsible 5. (v)olunteer

二、从方框中选择正确的短语并用正确的形式填空。(5小题,每题2分)
6. home and abroad 7. looking forward to 8. is skilled in 9. act as 10. major in

三、单项选择。(10小题,每题1分)
11-15 CABDA 16-20 DCBCD

四、语言应用。(5小题,每题2分)
21-25 BACCB

五、阅读理解。(15小题,每题2分)
26-30 BADCA 31-35 CBADD 36-40 BDACD

六、把左右栏相对应的句子匹配起来。(5小题,每题1分)
41-45 EDBAC

七、英汉互译。(15小题,每题2分)
46. 我在一所大学主修基础教育。
47. 北京故宫有600多年的历史,每年接待来自国内外的游客超过1900万人次。
48. 如果你有兴趣和热情,请在网上填写电子申请表。
49. 它的目的是感谢世界各地的志愿者奉献他们的时间和精力来帮助别人,并鼓励更多
52. was founded
53. three-party agreement
54. In order to; internship
55. make; progress
56. Did you check your insurance?
57. They also offer English courses to international students.
58. These courses provide high-level employment-related skills and knowledge.
59. Diplomas typically require one to two years of full-time study.
60. I finished my training plan.

的人做志愿者工作。
50. 多么重要的消息啊！
51. 时光飞逝！
52. look forward to
53. apply for
54. make new friends
55. are willing to
56. What an unforgettable experience it is!
57. Mike's hobby is collecting stamps.
58. I can teach children how to protect the sea.
59. We will consider your application and inform you of the result soon.
60. What responsible teachers they are!

期中检测题

一、单项选择。（每小题 1 分，共 15 分）
1-5 ACBBC   6-10 DCDCD   11-15 CBBAA
二、语言运用。（每小题 1.5 分，共 15 分）
16-20 CBAAC   21-25 BBBCA
三、阅读理解。（每小题 2 分，共 40 分）
26-30 CDCAB   31-35 ABCBB
36-40 CBACB   41-45 BABCB
四、补全对话。（每小题 1 分，共 5 分）
46-50 GEFCB
五、英汉互译。（每小题 2 分，共 10 分）
51. 我们可以和许多朋友友好地相处。
52. 我很高兴听到这件事，因为我很期待去看望我的爷爷。
53. 事实上，吸烟对人的健康有害。
54. make full use of
55. get rid of

六、书面表达。（共 15 分）
Shopping online is one of the most important shopping ways in our daily life. Some of us think that shopping online could save time and consumers could buy things whenever they want, it is convenient and cheap. However, others think that shopping online has some bad aspects due to following reasons: Firstly, the store online merely provide the pictures for consumers. Secondly, consumers can not check the quality of those products. Therefore, they lose the chance to enjoy shopping with their friends in person.

In my opinion, shopping online has more advantages than its drawbacks. Firstly, people could visit many stores, comparing the same product and find out the cheapest and best one to buy. Secondly, people could save much more time. Therefore, I believe that shopping online fascinates people a lot.

Unit 5 单元测试

一、根据首字母或中文意思完成句子。（5 小题，每题 1 分）
1.（a）ttractive   2.（c）haracter   3.（e）xhibition   4.（i）mpressed   5.（t）echnology
6. preparing for   7. date back to   8. As early as   9. Searched for   10. is influenced; by
二、从方框中选择正确的短语用正确的形式填空。（5 小题，每题 2 分）
三、单项选择。（10 小题，每题 1 分）
11-15 CDCAA   16-20 DABCC
四、语言应用。（5 小题，每题 2 分）
21-25 AABBB
五、阅读理解。（15 小题，每题 2 分）
26-30 BCBDB   31-35 BAACA   36-40 ACBBD
六、把左右栏相对的句子匹配起来。（5 小题，每题 1 分）
41-45 BEACD
七、英汉互译。（15 小题，每题 2 分）
46. 我们都对古希腊感兴趣。

Unit 6 单元测试

一、根据首字母或中文意思完成句子。(5小题，每题 1 分)

1. achieve 2. craftsmanship 3. creative 4. unique 5. persistent

二、从方框中选择正确的短语并用正确的形式填空。(5小题，每题 2 分)

6. focus on 7. Neither; nor 8. in the end 9. was/is connected to 10. take up

三、单项选择。(10小题，每题 1 分)

11-15: BCBDB 16-20 AABAC

四、语言应用。(5小题，每题 2 分)

21-25 ABCBB

五、阅读理解。(15小题，每题 2 分)

26-30 DAABC 31-35: BDACD

六、把左右栏相对应的句子匹配起来。(5小题，每题 1 分)

36-40 DACDB

41-45 CDBAE

七、英汉互译。(15小题，每题 2 分)

46. What qualities should the watchmakers have?
47. It is also important for them to be creative.
48. The skills were passed on from generation to generation at that time.
49. I believe that his experience is enough to take up this job.
50. Think twice before you do.
51. in person
52. take part
53. help laughing
54. once upon a time
55. strive for
56. "中国制造"的标签随处可见。
57. 剪纸是中国的一项传统技艺。
58. 这些房间每天都要打扫。
59. 2024年奥运会将在巴黎举办。
60. 万事开头难。

Unit 7 单元测试

一、根据首字母或中文意思完成句子。(5小题，每题 1 分)

1. (f)unction 2. (i)ntroduce 3. (p)refer 4. (d)oubtful 5. (w)arning

二、从方框中选择正确的短语并用正确的形式填空。(5小题，每题 2 分)

6. turn off 7. In the beginning 8. manage to 9. be used for 10. Online shopping

三、单项选择。(10小题，每题 1 分)

11-15 BCCDA 16-20 DDCAB

四、语言应用。(5小题，每题 2 分)

21-25 BCACA

五、阅读理解。(15小题，每题 2 分)

26-30 CDABB 31-35 DBCDC 36-40 CDABA

47. 他俩一见倾心。
48. 她的热情给我们留下了深刻的印象。
49. 这幅画是国宝。
50. 剪纸是中国最古老的民间艺术之一。
51. heard of
52. neither; nor
53. was sent to
54. takes; to
55. looking forward to
56. The ancient Silk Road has a long history.
57. Miss Zhang asked me why I was late for school.
58. The teacher told me the sun always rises in the east.
59. He doesn't know when she can come back.
60. Even today we are influenced by his ideas.

六、把右栏相对应的句子匹配起来。(5小题，每题1分)
41-45 CEABD

七、英汉互译。(15小题，每题2分)
46. 信不信由你，科技已给我们的生活带来了深刻的影响。
47. 科技创新在许多方面真正改变了我们的生活。
48. 网络上有各种各样的新闻和信息。
49. 网络是一种重要的通信手段。
50. 它能帮助农民检查庄稼的生长。
51. 这是最新产品，深受客户欢迎。
52. looking for
53. In my opinion
54. make; use of
55. in a way
56. What other sports do you like besides football?
57. Can you introduce yourself?
58. I prefer autumn to summer.
59. It took me one hour to go to the library by bus.
60. Hurry up, or you will be late for school.

Unit 8 单元测试

一、根据首字母或中文意思完成句子。(5小题，每题1分)
1. (P)rotect 2. (d)ropping 3. (r)ecyclable 4. (r)ealized 5. (r)estore

二、从方框中选择正确的短语并用正确的形式填空。(5小题，每题2分)
6. dried up 7. at the same time 8. Not until 9. Garbage sorting 10. Global warming

三、单项选择。(10小题，每题1分)
11-15 BBCBB   16-20 DDBDC

四、语言应用。(5小题，每题2分)
21-25 BCBCB

五、阅读理解。(15小题，每题2分)
26-30 BDCAB   31-35 CABCC   36-40 CBBAC

六、把右栏相对应的句子匹配起来。(5小题，每题1分)
41-45 BADCE

七、英汉互译。(15小题，每题2分)
46. 种树对我们人类是多么的重要和有用。
47. 保护地球环境是每一个人的责任。
48. 适合人类喝的水是越来越少了。
49. 没有人能离开水和空气生存。
50. 如果我们不节约水，那么最后一滴水也许会是我们人类的眼泪。
51. 保护树木，就是保护自己。
52. pretended; to
53. Whose; being
54. translated; into
55. felt; steal into
56. The child heard someone coming upstairs step by step.
57. How often do you have your room painted?
58. Did you make your clothes yourself or have them made?
59. Turn off the tap. Don't have the water running to waste!
60. The teachers don't let the children play on the grass.

期末检测题

第I卷（共两部分；满分70分）

第一部分 英语知识运用。（共两节；满分30分）

第一节 （共15小题；每小题1分，满分15分）
1-5 CABDB   6-10 CDCCD   11-15 ADCBB

第二节 （共10小题；每小题1.5分，满分15分）
16-20 BCBCB   21-25 BACAB

第二部分 阅读理解。(共 20 小题；每小题 2 分，满分 40 分)

26—30 DBACA 31—35 DBBAD

36—40 CCCAC 41—45 DADBB

第一节 朴全对话。(共 5 小题；每小题 1 分，满分 5 分)

46—50 GFCAB

第二节 英汉互译。(共 5 小题；每小题 2 分，满分 10 分)

51. 不要以貌取人。

52. 抱着足球的那个人是我的弟弟。

53. 比起出租车，我更喜欢坐公交车或地铁。

54. are strict with

55. rush hour

第Ⅱ卷(共 30 分)

第三节 书面表达。(满分 15 分)

参考范文：

How to Keep a Good Mood?

A good mood makes us comfortable and happy. However, it's not easy to keep a good mood, especially when we are faced with trouble. Then, how can we keep a good mood?

To begin with, we should keep healthy. It's known to us that a weak body always has a negative effect on our mood. Secondly, we had better have a good rest, which plays a very important role in maintaining our mental health. Thirdly, it's of great benefit to recall those which make us happy. Memories of those things contribute to a good mood. Lastly, think the positive aspect of everything. Don't live a life full of worries. Only by doing these can we keep a good mood.